MW01639700

BRIDGE BUILDER'S GUIDE

Kyle Ferlemann

A study companion for
the degrees of the
Southern Jurisdiction of
the Ancient and Accepted
Scottish Rite Masonry

Bridge Builder's Guide

A Cornerstone Book
Published by Cornerstone Book Publishers
An Imprint of Michael Poll Publishing

Cornerstone Book Publishers
New Orleans, LA
www.cornerstonepublishers.com

Part of the Cornerstone Scottish Rite Education Series

First Cornerstone Edition - 2012

ISBN: 1613420439
ISBN 13: 978-1-61342-043-0

MADE IN THE USA

32
SPES MEA IN DEO EST
®

ACKNOWLEDGEMENTS:

I would be remiss if I did not recognize the people who were instrumental in the creation and refinement of this book. Expressly to my wise and calm, proof reading wife who has read this book as many time as I have, to my mother, with her years as an editor, and my brothers in the Valley who helped me work out the puzzlers; I give my deepest gratitude. The leadership of my Valley and Orient were beyond supportive and most insightful in helping align the book to the real needs of the Scottish Rite. That kind of vision is rare and wonderful. Thanks to the scholarly writers of Masonry who all said it was OK to think big. Special thanks go to the leadership and staff at the House of the Temple who provided not just encouragement but real support in this endeavor.

TABLE OF CONTENTS

INTRODUCTION

This text is the result of the search for light. The articles herein are not final conclusions but the author's observations of the writings of other older and better teachers. To quote Brother Pike: "He claims no greater understanding of Masonry or the study of Masonry. Everyone is entirely free to reject or dissent from whatsoever herein may seem to him to be untrue or unsound. It is only required of him that he shall weigh what is taught, and give it fair hearing and unprejudiced judgment.[1]" As described in the Royal Arch of Solomon, the clues lead us ever forward to the truth, even though at first we may not recognize what we have found.

This book does not answer questions, it places them in context. You will find many connections and lessons that are not identified in this book; this is intentional. The degrees are very strong on their own and will show you a definitive path. This text will help you recognize the signs along the way.

The Song of Liberty:

Within any study of Masonry through the Scottish Rite University of Free Masonry there is to be found a wealth of information on individual spiritual and moral development, effective social interaction, philosophical exploration, religious ideals, political introduction to the tenets of liberty, and exposure to the history and development of the liberal arts and sciences; all set within the frame work of the call to duty, timeliness, and zeal. Each of us as individuals takes from Masonry something different. It is like listening to music. Some hear a beat or a rhythm, others a melody or a chorus. In time we all come to recognize it to be the Song of Liberty.

The lessons of the degrees and the meanings of the symbols have been well explained. Wise and learned men understand them and teach them to new Masons every day, but there is something more. Preserved within them is a tapestry so intricate, so cunning, so complete, that its depth has been lost to many; not because of some shortcoming on the part of the Masonic mentors but because a man could take the overt lessons of Freemasonry, grow wise and just, and be completely satisfied.

As satisfying as these lessons may be, there is a greater tutorial within the degrees; not just to make good men better but to teach the ultimate course of personal development, civics, and politics. This is done through direct messages and subtle themes. The messages, or specific lessons of the degrees, are all solid lessons and can stand alone as a series of separate lessons. But there is, in fact, much more to the degrees. Within the messages are also themes. Themes being ideas that are addressed subtly, as part of the message of the degree, which are introduced incrementally throughout several degrees so as to relate a complex concept in a manner that makes them seem only natural when finally revealed.

The true mission of the Masons:

This course of instruction has a specific purpose. "The province of Masonry is to teach a path to all forms of truth – moral, political, philosophical, and religious.[2]" To create within the free world a host of men who are capable of recognizing and defending freedom from the myriad aggressors who would see freedom fail in the advancement of their own interests. This is not a modern conspiracy theory; this is a time-tested, and often repeated, lesson of history.

The Rational:

The best chance freedom has is if there are within each city, town, and county men who are morally and spiritually fit, educated in the history of freedom and able to recognize the erosion of Liberty, learned in the liberal arts and sciences, proficient in the articulation of philosophy, supported within a strong and durable social support structure, capable of recognizing genuinely like-minded men, and most importantly, willing to accept the responsibility of acting in the defense of Liberty when it is threatened.

The Methodology:

This is why we are Knights. This is why we swear the five oaths of the thirty-second degree[3]. The benefit is that in the process of preparing for the worst we learn things that are just as useful in times of peace as in times of conflict. In this way Masons prepare for the preservation of peace, identify and dissuade intolerance, superstition, and bigotry before they fester and mature into fanaticism, despotism and ignorance.

Our hope is with God, our trust is in the wisdom of the ages, our strength is in our willingness to serve, but our success is on our actions. To this end the author humbly submits this articulation of the lesson plans of the degrees. Set out in guided explanation so mentors can provide the lessons more effectively and so students can set the degrees in a perspective to better comprehend and internalize the varied messages and themes therein.

This is done to fill the void we currently encounter between the methods of the past and the current presentation of the degrees. Through the passing of the years we have lost something of the teachings due to lack of time, resources, and men to teach. The degrees have, in many cases, transformed from lessons into ceremonies and traditions, and in so doing some of the lesson may be lost.

"No better means could be devised to rouse a dormant intellect, than those impressive exhibitions, which addressed it through the imagination; which, instead of condemning it to a proscribed routine of creed, invited it to seek, compare, and judge. The alteration from the symbol to dogma is as fatal to beauty of expression, as that from faith to dogma is to truth and wholesomeness of thought.[4]"

Recognizing that we will most likely not return to the preferred method of full degree presentations any time soon we must preserve the messages and themes of the degrees in the context of the complete framework of the Masonic tutorial or risk losing the depth of their meaning.

Do not blindly translate these degrees out of tradition or un-thoughtful memorization. Masonic mentors must first seek out the meaning and truths within the philosophies of Masonry. Only when those lessons are internalized and understood, in the context of the complete Masonic education that is imbedded within the degrees, will the teacher be able to effectively articulate to the student the full meaning of the degrees and the relevance of the symbols associated with them.

The Framework:

Set out within this text is the framework of the Masonic Tutorage of the Scottish Rite, the relationship of the messages to the themes are explained, the representative symbols are illuminated, and the building of the man shown within a defined set of developmental goals. This text does not claim to identify every separate lesson to be found in Masonry, only the frame work in which the lessons are arranged.

This book does not represent a different or new idea but rather articulates the fullness of the degrees. Everything has been laid down before by wise men for us to discover. This is the articulation of their plan, the explanation of their rational, and the revelation of their true Masonic goal. It is important that we study with the full knowledge of what we want to accomplish. Masons should not seek random secrets for the promotion of their individual situation but instead seek the fullness of true illumination so that they may better serve their fellow man. The

Bridge to Light can be fraught with perils for those who misinterpret the symbols. We are repeatedly warned of this because the lessons are difficult and complex. The Bridge to Light must be built according to plan.

For students of Masonry and their Mentors, this is the *Bridge Builder's Guide*.

Kyle Ferlemann
2012

FOREWORD

One can never have too many resources when it comes to interpreting the lessons embedded within the degrees of the Scottish Rite. There are so many lessons. The Scottish Rite is not called the college course in Freemasonry because it has imposing temples scattered about the urban landscape. It is an advanced field of Masonic study. There are many lessons to be learned. It is a course in principles and situational ethics, comparative religion, the ancient mysteries, the traditions of manhood, and the psychology of being. Like any other knowledge tradition, the value one gains from its lessons expands dramatically as these are applied in life. The Scottish Rite, more than any other fraternal discipline, focuses on the nature of freedom: individual, religious, political, and spiritual liberty. The moral, social, and spiritual development of the individual is the foundational criteria for freedom. Thus, the importance of the Rite should never be taken for granted.

A *Bridge Builder's Guide* is an apt name for the textual path this book offers the student of Masonry. It recognizes one of the greatest challenges the new Scottish Rite Mason encounters: how one goes about studying and thinking about the Degrees of the Rite when he has only an occasional opportunity to observe them. Informational bridges are needed to connect the Mason to the major themes presented in the Rite to help him on his individual path of study toward enlightenment. Brother Ferlemann offers us an excellent tutorial for exploring the truths and philosophies of our great work.

Separating Masonic study into its three essential components of ceremonial art, social engineering, and symbolic interpretation is nothing short of brilliant. One has to know what truth is before he can approach a meaningful study of its nature. He has to understand the personal, social, and political messages the Rite conveys to decipher the true nature of liberty. He has to have a grasp of the major themes and characters presented in the Degrees to interpret the applications its ceremonial forms has to him.

This study offers the student much foundational information for interpreting the major elements of Scottish Rite philosophy. It provides an important framework for a more efficient and meaningful exploration of the nature of freedom. It helps bridge the gap between the philosophy of ideas and real world application. It places each of us, as the central characters in its Degrees, on the path to improve ourselves and the world in which we live.

It is my pleasure to welcome you on Brother Ferlemann's enjoyable journey from whence we came to wither we are travelling. I can assure you it is a bridge worth crossing.

Robert G. Davis, 33°, G.C.
Guthrie, Oklahoma
2012

BRIDGE BUILDER'S GUIDE

PART ONE:

DO UNTO OTHERS AS YOU WOULD HAVE OTHERS DO UNTO YOU

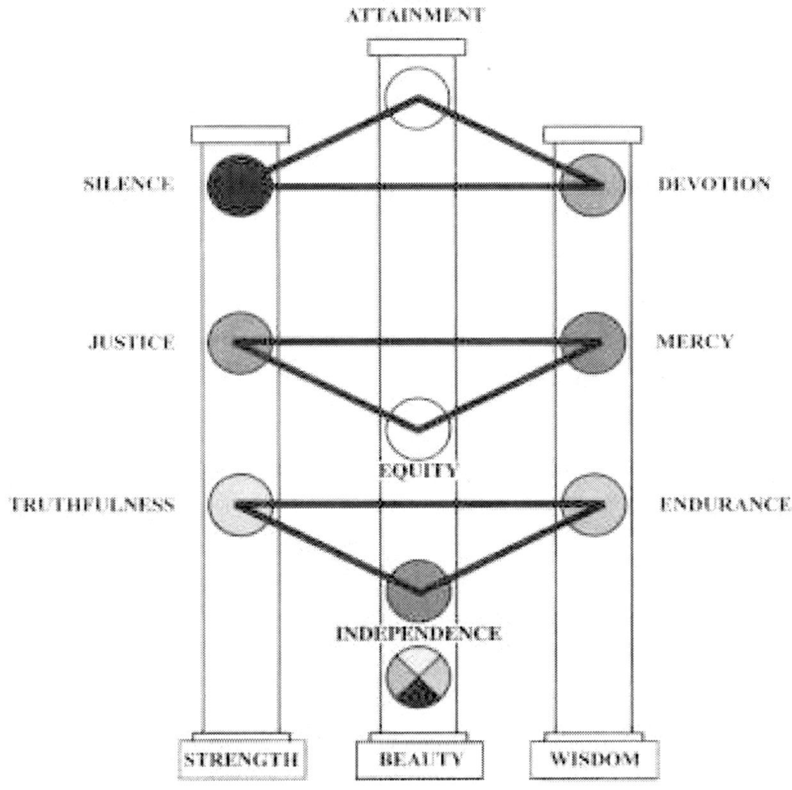

CHAPTER ONE:
MASONIC STUDY

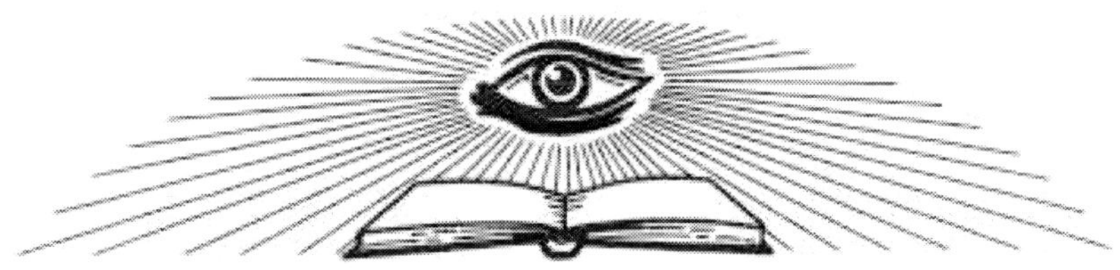

First and foremost, before you read any further, understand that the Scottish Rite is the University of Free Masonry. To study and grow in Masonry you MUST read. Seek and consume the texts and ideas of those fine scholars or tragic fools who came before you and learn from both their triumph and their folly. Strive to understand what they knew and build upon their lifetimes of knowledge. A good place to start is the various Masonic Research Societies, if only because they are one of the best and most accessible sources of relevant material on Masonry. The annual publication of Heredom from the Scottish Rite Research Society has essays and articles to answer your questions or lead you closer to answers. It is still only a place to start.

Within the University of Free Masonry there are three general areas of study. Each is important and required for overall success in the study of Scottish Rite Masonry. These are Ceremonial Arts, Social Engineering, and Esoteric Studies. The in-depth study of Masonry can be difficult, time consuming work and not everyone will reach complete understanding. As difficult as this assessment may be to accept, the reality is that many modern Masons simply do not understand the full extent of what Masonry has to offer. It is social but it is not a social club, it studies religions but is not a religion itself, it teaches political tenets but is not a political movement. What Masonry is, in fact, is a learning tool for those who seek the light of truth in religion, politics and social virtue. The purpose of Masonry is to teach and promote study in the ways of right thinking, right speech and right action. A prudent approach to Scottish Rite study is to develop a sound understanding of each of these three general areas, even if you chose to concentrate on only one of them.

Each area of study provides insights and ideals which support the other two. The ceremonies preserve the messages of Masonry. These messages include social engineering which preserves Liberty, and introduction to esoteric themes which promote the study of man's relationship with Deity. In order for individual Masons to enjoy the freedom to illuminate their souls they must create a free society in which all people may enjoy religious and intellectual freedom.

Ceremonial Arts

The Ceremonial Arts are the theater of Scottish Rite Masonry. The reading and study of the degrees after the ceremonies have been observed is not what is addressed here. The Ceremonial Arts are specifically the presentation and communication of the degrees. Albert Pike's vision of the presentation of the degrees did not include stage presentation.[5] With very little exception he believed the degrees should be conducted in a lodge room setting with sashes and jewels signifying the respective characters. In the mid 1800's theatrical methods became more prominent, first in the Northern Jurisdiction and then later in the Southern Jurisdiction, after Pike's passing.[6] But in both the Lodge and the theater setting the importance of the *presentation* of the degrees cannot be emphasized enough. The costumes, props, make-up, sets, lighting, and recited word is how Masonry came to be taught. There was a time when it was not uncommon for men to weep or even faint from the majesty, strength, and magnitude of the degree presentations.

"No better means could be devised to rouse a dormant intellect, than those impressive exhibitions, which addressed it through the imagination; which, instead of condemning it to a proscribed routine of creed, invited it to seek, compare, and judge. The alteration from the symbol to dogma is as fatal to beauty of expression, as that from faith to dogma is to truth and wholesomeness of thought."[7] This is in keeping with the traditions of the Mystery Schools which believed that true learning can only come from experience.

The Ceremonies of Masonry are the receptacle of all we know. More importantly they are designed to be the method by which we *teach* Masonry. They exist for the preservation of the ancient truths in an exact form so even as the understanding of the lessons may wax and wane, the message itself is preserved. The droning memorization which brings forth so many complaints is in fact the real meat and potatoes of what Masonry has to teach. Many of the messages in the degrees are difficult to understand because they have multiple meanings and many degrees "direct" candidates to knowledge they should seek rather than "providing" it. This is done with a specific and very important intent: to require the study of the ideals represented in the degrees according to a *lesson plan*. The purpose of this lesson plan is not only to encourage the Mason to study but to lead the Mason through the thought process of learning by introducing ideas incrementally and sequentially.

This is heady stuff; personal development and wisdom, the tenets of effective free governance, the nature of divinity and the name of God. A lot of what Masonry has to offer is very difficult to grasp conceptually: first, because these concepts can be very different from the social or political norm, and second, because the ideals and applications are truly complex. When we study the lessons of Masonry out of context we may get the information, but miss the point! The current confusion of information resulting from the myriad books on Masonry, Hermetic thought, Alchemy, History, and other related subjects is a direct result of the loss of academic direction resulting from not recognizing the study guide provided by the ceremonies.

Originally, Albert Pike's vision was that degrees would be presented one or two a year and conducted in their resplendent entirety with the recipient of the degree participating as the candidate elect.[8] This was so the candidate would experience, first hand, the message of each degree and have time for the contemplation of its meaning. Mentors would be readily available and well versed in the lessons and their meanings.

The reality was that most Valleys never performed all of the degrees but communicated most of them. They relied on a small list of "indispensable" degrees for presentation.[9] Only a few select degees were performed and in too many cases they were conducted with much of the original content removed, characters were deleted, and lesson continuity was lost. For years before the turn of the century in 2000 it was common to have a variety of different versions of the degrees performed across the Southern Jurisdiction. Most of the revisions were made at the Orient or state level, but it was not uncommon for Valleys to have their own adaptation of the degrees.

The regrettable result is that through the passing of the years, due to lack of time, resources, and men who read and teach we have lost something of the teachings. In the time of Albert Pike the degrees would take several hours to perform.[10] As time became an issue parts of the degrees were simply dropped from the presentation. The degrees were unknowingly being transformed from lessons into incomprehensible ceremonies and misunderstood traditions, and in so doing many of the lessons were lost. The idea that a play can fail to properly convey a message is not a new concern. Even Shakespeare apologies to his audience in Henry V for the reduction of so great an event as the battle of Agincourt to what he described as "a brawl ridiculous".

Recognizing that most Valleys will not return to complete degree performances in the traditional method, those who perform the ceremonies must endeavor to preserve the messages and themes of the degrees in the context of the complete framework of the Masonic tutorial or they too will risk losing the depth of their meaning. In the late 90's and early 2000's there were many efforts to rewrite the degrees in order to recapture their meaning in a shorter and more presentable program. For the sake of uniformity the supreme council, Southern Jurisdiction elected to commission Dr. Rex Hutchens to rewrite the degrees for an new official version which was released in 2004. The rewrite efforts remained true to the lessons and tenets envisioned by Albert Pike.

Without the context and sequence provided by the ceremonies, the study of Masonry loses its focus and the chances of recognizing and understanding the important lessons are reduced dramatically. The Ceremonial Arts can now be studied uniformly within Scottish Rite Masonry because the Supreme Council, Ancient and Accepted Scottish Rite, Southern Jurisdiction, Mother Council of the World has provided us with a standard for the Ceremonies (currently 2004).

An important point in all of this is the fact that most Scottish Rite Masons, no matter the generation they were born into, received their degrees mostly through Communication. Communication is an explanation or reading of the degree. A lucky few have had the opportunity to see the indispensable degrees performed in Lodge or on stage and fewer still have ever seen all of the degrees performed in full. Should you find yourself a little confused as to the how and why of the presentation of the degrees, do not be discouraged. The truth is, with some exceptions, modern Scottish Rite Masons have a greater chance of seeing the degrees performed that in days past. I highly recommend that you attend your Valley's Reunions to watch the degree presentations. If they do not perform them in your Valley, find a Valley where the ceremonies are performed. If you have the opportunity to participate in the presentation of the degree ceremonies, do it. It is a valuable learning experience and worth the endeavor.

Social Engineering

In Social Engineering we study three aspects of Liberty; the promotion of personal development in order to become a productive citizen; the tenets of a free society so we can understand and articulate the benefits of freedom; and the political methods used to sustain a government of the people, by the people, and for the people.

These lessons are delivered through direct messages and subtle themes. The messages, or specific lessons of the degrees, are all solid lessons and can stand alone as a string of separate lessons. But there is, in fact, much more to the degrees. Within the messages are also themes. Themes being ideas that are addressed subtly, as part of the message of the degree, which are introduced incrementally throughout several degrees so as to relate a complex concept in a manner that makes them seem only natural when finally revealed.

The respective goals of the bodies are reflected in a series of developmental and instructional degrees within the Lodge of Perfection and the Chapter of Rose Croix, followed by instruction in chivalric law and philosophy within the Council of Kadosh, and concluded with a judicial tutorial in the Consistory. A cursory review of the bodies is provided here. Use these notes to assist you in putting the lessons of the degrees into context.

The Lodge of Perfection is focused on the growth of the Individual. Within its degrees the Mason builds his personal Temple by learning what "right" looks like.

Degrees 4-6, Call to Duty with prompt Action and Zeal
Degrees 7-11, Tenets of Justice and the responsibility of Stewardship
Degrees 12-14, The importance and application of Education, and the Mastery of Self

The Chapter of Rose Croix is a short but powerful explanation that the call to service is really a call to serve mankind. The Rose Croix degrees offer a transformation of how the Mason sees himself and his interactions with the world around him. He learns that there is a place in society for men who can affect what "right" looks like and that he may be one of these men once he acquires the skills to be so.

Degrees 15-16, Call to service for Mankind
Degrees 17-18, Transformation of the Mason into a man among men

The Council of Kadosh is the formal education of the aspirant Knight. These chivalric and philosophical lessons take the Mason through his initial apprenticeship to the first of several possible avenues of adeptness. Some doors open, some doors are only alluded to. Here a Mason learns the methods and wisdom of affecting what "right" looks like.

Degrees 19-22, Chivalric duties and codes of conduct
Degrees 23-26, Introduction to the Mysteries, which are the philosophies of the great religions.
Degrees 27-30, Knighthood, The call to service as a Leader of Men

The Consistory is a tutorial in the application of Justice. Here a man learns how to make things "right" through the application of man's law, which is our humble attempt to mimic God's Justice.

Degrees 31-32, Methods and application of Justice

All this is done within the time honored story line of the Hero's Quest.[11] The candidate discovers there is a great mystery. He seeks knowledge and joins with comrades to train and prepare. He departs on a quest and finds himself alone, destitute, and care worn. When he is at his weakest he is confronted with his greatest trial. He discovers the truth is before his eyes and his goal is within his grasp but until he sheds his fear of death and personal weaknesses he is bound, blind, and lost. In the end he discovers that wisdom, strength, and beauty are found in compassion, tolerance, and Mastery of Self; this is the true victory. Or if you prefer the Alchemical tradition: The burning away of the selfish and worldly, the refinement and purification of the soul, and the transformation of the soul to a higher state through the recognition or application of a higher power. The story of transformation is essentially the same.

Esoteric Studies

This consists of the individual search for truth in the hermetic traditions, the study of religions, myth, alchemy, and the Kabbalah. These studies can be a quagmire of symbols, ideas, allegories, and purposeful misdirection. The degree ceremonies offer a progressive and steady introduction to esoteric themes and it is prudent and helpful to follow the recommended introductions provided by them. The Ceremonies and Scottish Rite bodies also offer a place to categorize, organize, and relate much of the knowledge which is found in esoteric study. With reflection one will find that many esoteric lessons relate back to the civic, social, and political aspects. This is important. All esoteric study is related to man's relationship with the Divine. This is expressed in knowledge of self and knowledge of nature. Man's relationship with humanity and with nature is a direct reflection of man's relationship with Deity. These are not separate ideas and concepts; and to deny one aspect isolates the student from adeptness in the other.

Because esoteric study has been banned out-right for much of recorded history it is important to keep the lessons of Social Engineering in mind and remember not to immerse oneself too deeply or too separately into Esoteric Studies as this will tend to blind the student to the world around him. Consider the fear and distrust of alchemy held by both clergy and kings. This distrust was not always based in tyranny. Alchemists wanted freedom of thought, separate from religious constraint, in order to facilitate discovery and create change. If you were a king, would you want the fellow who could make the best metals for weapons and who could create gun powder to be a radical thinker or someone who was disinterested in social stability? Realize the search for knowledge is as inherently dangerous as it is worthwhile. Knowledge in and of itself is neutral, its use or application depends upon the user and can either be for good or ill.

As for specifics, there is no need for me to add to the abundant variety of texts on the Hermetic traditions. I offer here only a method to organize the dizzying plethora of ideas, opinions, and theories so that, by comparison, the valid aspects might be more easily identified and their respective meaning better understood.

Kabbalah: The Kabbalah is one of many forms of mysticism; the study of man's relationship with Deity.[12] In mysticism man seeks union with God through having a better understanding of God's plan. An example of mysticism is Numerology which focuses on using numbers and dates associated with a person to "determine" that individual's disposition and future according to "God's Plan".

For study of the Kabbalah the best references are the mystic books of the Hebrew faith which include the Sefir Yetzirah, the Sefir Zohar, and the Sefir Bahir. The secret is not hidden; the secret is the Kabbalistic tree. If you try to look past the tree you will miss what it has to say. Read and re-read the meanings of the Sephiroth and understand the pillars. Understanding the contradictions is not the hard part. Living a life of balance within the contradictions is. Although it is helpful to read commentary from the studies others have made on the Kabbalistic tree, do not rely too heavily on any one. Read several and blend the interpretations. Find the common thread among several authors to avoid being drawn away from the core lessons which constitute the real treasures offered by the Kabbalah.

Alchemy: The goal of alchemy is an inward process, the perfecting of the individual and the immortalization of the Soul.[13] There are several areas of study within alchemy but generally they can be expressed in two aspects; alchemy as a precursor to chemistry, and alchemy as transformation of the human soul.

Alchemy as a precursor to chemistry can be confusing because of all the different names for the respective elements and chemicals and what is done with them to make desired changes. Most acids and effecting compounds were believed to be derivatives of salt, sulfur, and mercury which corresponded to the elements of earth, air, water, and fire. Remember that early chemists had to distill all of their own materials and that it was very important to them that the individual alchemist "put himself" into the process. This meant that if you did not do all the work yourself the transformation process would not work.

There are 12 core alchemical processes and 109 unique processes for changing elements.[14] The knowledge of how to make these changes was closely guarded by practitioners and often resulted in very confusing explanations. This was because in many cases they purposely disguised or encoded the meaning of their descriptions so that only certain people would understand what was written. Most of these mystery substances can now be found in any local hardware store or high school chemistry laboratory. Remember that there is no magic here. Alchemy as transformation of the human soul has proven to be more difficult to describe. This is true for two core reasons. First, because of religious repression, the process of self awareness was highly discouraged and second, due to that repression, the early esoteric writings on how to accomplish self-awareness were disguised or encoded. In many cases meditative processes were referred to in chemical terms thus confusing the study of the chemical arts with those of progressive spiritual thinking. To assist in separating the two keep these ideas in mind.

Chemical alchemy had to do with the refinement of elements to their base, or purest, forms. This included reducing salts to acids, and mixed minerals to base metals. These processes were referred to as reduction and purification; or blackening and whitening. There are hundreds of texts addressing this from across the span of time. Understand that early chemistry and medicine were not separated from spiritual studies. They were considered to be interchangeable.

It is when the texts start referring to transformation, or reddening, sometimes with a substance referred to as Philosophers stone, that the authors were then addressing spiritual growth and "purification of the soul". A good example of this is The Book of Lambspring by Nicholas Barnaud Delphinas.[15] Although it is an alchemical text it is referring directly to spiritual understanding and personal growth.

How to study Masonry

In the study of Masonry there are several gems of guidance, which for the most part go un-heralded or un-recognized. The phrase "To know, to will, to dare, and to be silent"[16] is one of them. It is a synthesis of what it means to be a Mason. Like any other symbol it is an enigma that does not lend itself to being easily understood. Without some prior knowledge one would not know what to study, what should be done with audacity, how to dare, or what pitfalls to avoid. Even after one is well established in Masonic education, the phrase requires and deserves considerable contemplation.

The key to the phrase is found in taking it apart and putting it back together, "solve et coagula", analyze and synthesize. Because words mean something they can reveal the meaning of "to know, to will, to dare, and to be silent".

To KNOW is to commit yourself to the advancement of your mental condition. This is not just the mere collection of information to facilitate mental gymnastics. We are instructed to be the intellect enlightened by study. Intellect is the ability to think, reason, and understand. Enlightened is to be rational and free of ignorance, prejudice, or superstition. Study is to learn about a subject through reading, research and contemplation. If these definitions are true then an intellect enlightened by study reads, researches and learns in order to be free of ignorance, prejudice, or superstition with the intended purpose of being able to think, reason, and understand. This ability to think freely is a prerequisite to the next aspect.

To WILL is to let nothing stop you from attaining your goals, to possess an audacity which nothing checks. This requires fearlessness because audacity is a daring or willingness to challenge assumptions or conventions or tackle something difficult or dangerous. There is a pitfall involved with audacity as it also includes an aspect of arrogant disregard for personal safety, conventional thought, or social restrictions. Just because you do not need the permission of others to have your own ideas does not mean you may treat those individuals with disrespect. A prudent man would listen to what they have to say, thank them, consider the options and then continue on his path with the due warning in mind. Audacity is beautifully bold but arrogance is folly.

To DARE is to possess the will that nothing can conquer. If daring is the mental faculty by which one deliberately chooses or decides upon a course of action then it translates specifically to the ability to make a decision and act upon it. This may seem like Will but it is really something more. Daring is the ability to begin, to commitment to the act itself.

To be SILENT is to have discretion that nothing may corrupt or intoxicate. This is a tough aspect and may be one most difficult to master. This does not mean we are easily corruptible. It does mean that there is a pitfall we must avoid. Discretion includes not just authority but also tact and confidentiality. Even with the power or right to decide and act according to one's own desire, one must possess the good judgment and sensitivity needed to avoid embarrassing or upsetting others, and most importantly, the ability to keep sensitive information secret.

What we do as Masons is not for everyone and you must always remember that you decided to seek enlightenment on your own. Those who are not seeking enlightenment may well find your ideas strange or even threatening. One of the aspects of Masonry is to teach others to be free of tyranny, despotism, and ignorance. You cannot give a man freedom. He must want it and seek it on his own. The truth is that people like the illusion their ignorance provides and it is not our place to force reality on anyone who is incapable, unwilling, or disinterested in accepting the aspects of enlightenment we study in Masonry.

Remember that the things you love most are not the same as what another man may love and want.

To know, to will, to dare, and to be silent is both a directive and a warning. The more you study Masonry the more distant you become from the bulk of humanity. As you become a Soldier of the Light, a Soldier of Liberty, and a Soldier of the People you will become more than what you were before. As a Soldier of the Scottish Rite you will be required to know things others do not want to know and to do things for others that they do not want to do for themselves. This is the nature of the Five Vows you will encounter in the 32nd degree. Are you willing to be different than those around you? More importantly, are you willing to be different than you are now?

Conclusion: The study of any or all of these areas will lead the student to a series of contradictions. These contradictions represent a truth. The truth is that although some things are certain, nothing is absolute, and balance is required in all things. This is the lesson of equilibrium found in the 32nd degree. This same concept is found equally within the study of the Scottish Rite ceremonies where the truth is hidden in plain sight, in the study of the degrees where the maintenance of social order is required before individual freedom of thought can blossom to its fullest potential, and in esoteric study were the physical laws of nature define and reflect the beauty of Divinity. Each area of study is both unique in itself while also being dependent upon the others in order to be understood in context.

CHAPTER TWO: WHO ARE THE BAD GUYS AND WHY SHOULD WE CARE?

There is a theme within Masonry that a careful scholar will find with regularity. Masonry rarely judges the man. It instead judges actions of men and the individual is left to judge himself against that standard. When the individual changes his motivations and behavior from selfish to contributory, although still responsible and accountable for his past actions, his transgressions are left in the past. A careful study of the degrees will reveal that there are no specific references to personal evils in Masonry. Personal behavior is addressed in reference to positive aspects of behavior (Virtues) as opposed to the negative (Sins). Because men come to Masonry seeking enlightenment, threats of damnation and other uses of fear are unnecessary to motivate their participation. This means that within the degrees you will not find implicit instruction on the avoidance of sin. What you will find are examples of moral virtue which, through understanding and emulation, will help you become a better person.

Masonry teaches us to meet on the level, act on the plumb, and part on the square. By mastering the passions through moderation, being tolerant, charitable, humble, generous, and forgiving of the transgressions of others the student will find that he has avoided undue pride, covetousness, envy, gluttony, undue anger, idleness, lust, cruelty, malevolence, hypocrisy, and ingratitude. Masonry does not demand compliance but rather encourages improvement.

The goal is enlightenment. It is not enough just to stop selfish or destructive behavior by intimidation or brute force. The best and surest way to stop a man from being selfish and destructive is to change his motivations; to help him lose his fear and anger and let him become someone who does not want to do harm. Hate the sin not the sinner, remove the sin and save the man. Some transgressions are too much to bear. Murder, rape, and treason are examples of transgressions that may be too great to overcome. It is not for Masonry to judge such men; the laws of the community will do that. We are mostly concerned with assisting those who chose to seek enlightenment and are capable of the journey.

What Masonry identifies as "the enemy" are those things that would keep a man from finding enlightenment.[17] This includes anything that would deny a man his freedom, his liberty, or his right to live as he sees fit as long as he does not infringe on the rights of others. Masonry expresses, and history confirms, that the three things most likely to deny enlightenment are fanaticism, despotism and ignorance.

Fanaticism refers to the motivations and actions of those who follow a political or spiritual ideal with an extreme and uncritical zeal, dedication, or enthusiasm. Fanaticism is irrational and often focuses attention on compliance to unrealistically strict requirements by all persons, whether they are associated with the belief system or not.

Despotism refers to the motivations and actions of those who claim political and spiritual authority and use cruelty and injustice in the exercise of power or authority over others in order to control their actions and thoughts. This aspect is defined as Despotism when a single entity or group rules with absolute power. It is called Tyranny when the methods of Despotism are made systematic. They are twin ideals of malice and never far apart.

Ignorance refers to an inability or unwillingness to know or perceive something of importance. It also comprises two other aspects: a lack of desire to discover what is important and worth knowing, even when faced with an emergency or conflict; and active denial, an aggressive resistance to anyone who may challenge a belief held in ignorance. Where fanaticism is an absolute belief, ignorance is an absolute denial.

This can be visualized by three concentric circles with the inner circle being the tyrant who commands, the second circle being the fanatic who follows blindly, and the outer circle being the ignorant who do not question. In Masonry these three threats to freedom, liberty, and enlightenment are embodied in the persons of Jubelo, Jubela, and Jubelum.

Jubela-Guibs is the first ruffian who was a conspirator in the death of the Grand Master. He represents fanaticism and those forces which seek to silence a man's voice. For this reason he strikes with a 24 inch gauge. The 24 inch gauge is symbolic of a rule, law, or canon (religious rule or law) which seeks to deny a man the right to free expression.[18]

Jubelo-Gravelot is the second ruffian who was a conspirator in the horrid scheme. He represents despotism and those forces which seek to control the hearts of men. For this reason he strikes with a square. The square in this case is symbolic of political and religious law combined in one leader. The two edges come together to form a point which strikes at the heart of man and seeks to deny a man his freedom of choice.[19]

Jubelum-Akirop is the third ruffian and conspirator who dealt the death blow to the Grand Master. He represents ignorance and those forces that deny a man the right to learn and think on his own. For this reason he strikes with a setting maul. The Setting maul is symbolic of the bluntness of ignorance. It is the blunt force which unseats the light of intellect from the mind keeping men ignorant. [20]

There is a fourth villain to guard against and that is our own weakness; our own tendency to feel we are better suited to think for another man than he is himself, which is a form of despotism. Whenever we accept what we are told without question until our own beliefs become blind superstitions, we succumb to fanaticism; to surrender to the ease of letting another man manage our liberty, or to desire the bliss of not having to know rather than the responsibility of learning and thinking for ourselves; this is ignorance.

If we as Masons do not recognize and combat these dangers darkness will overcome us and we will be denied the opportunity to live free and study our relationship with Deity. Succumbing to them literally keep us from learning, thinking, speaking, or living freely. Historical examples abound. Not just in the distant past but within our lifetimes. Hitler's Germany, Stalin's Russia, and Mao's China are not so far away.

These ideas of fanaticism, despotism and ignorance are the opposites of the enlightenment offered in Masonry. Those who are motivated by these ideas are willing or unknowing foes of enlightenment and Masonry. The degrees of the Scottish Rite are full of references to each of these dangers and provide excellent examples of the manifestation of each.

The degrees also provide equally useful counters-measures. We must understand that the real threats to Masonry and enlightenment are not the individuals who perpetrate these evils. If one villain is removed another will always rise to take his place. The true danger is man's willingness to live in darkness by submitting to fear and anger, and the ease of letting others do for us what we should do for ourselves. Masons seek to promote a stable representative republic where these evils will find little opportunity to grow. Of course, Masons are not the only people in the world who want freedom and peace. But look to any struggle for freedom and you find Masons engaged in ways, both subtle and overt, against fanaticism, despotism and ignorance.

For specific examples of how to combat the darkness see the vows of the 32nd degree.

CHAPTER THREE: HOW DO WE TELL IF SOMETHING IS TRUE?

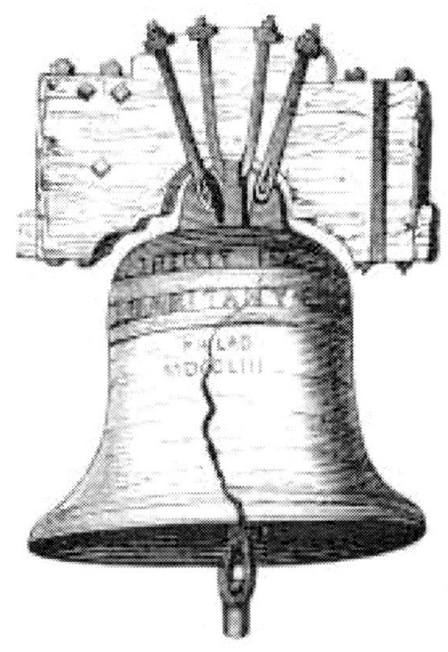

True is a strange and enigmatic word. There are many things that are factually correct that are said to be true. For the sake of semantics separate those things which are fact from those things that are true. A fact is a single quantifiable statement which stands alone without respect to other information, 2 + 2 = 4 is a fact. A truth is a number of separate facts set within a set of circumstances; a situation. This makes the truth less quantifiable, more subjective, harder to define and easier to confuse. That freedom is better for a nation than tyranny is true. In some cases free nations have risen on this truth, in others men have killed to conceal and deny this truth, claiming that only their authoritarian rule was correct for the good of all.

So how do we tell if something is true? First we must realize that it takes time to determine the truth. The lies of despots reveal themselves in the fullness of time. We do we not see the truth easily because truth is not one fact or aspect. A fact can be true and still be representative of a falsehood or lie of omission. Only by experience can we come to understand the relationship between the fact and the situation. Even with experience, wisdom and the willingness to accept the reality of a truth are required before we can gain insight to what is true.

Contradictions abound. Reality is not affected by our desires, but truth is. One must separate himself from what he wants in order to see the truth of his desires. For our perception of truth to be clear our desires must be based within the realm of the feasible, the scale of the probable, and the confines of the reasonable. This is not consistent with a human behavior model which is dominated by denial and careless justification. Even if we do these things correctly, our first realization of truth may not be complete. Perception of truth takes time. Why is this so hard? Why is it not natural?

Truth is not natural. There is no truth in nature. Nature is not true, it is real. Nature is above truth, neither false nor true, it is what it is; no more and no less. If there is no truth in nature then truth must be an aspect of the individual mind. If truth is an aspect of the individual then the only truths are those motivations realized, rationalized, denied, or un-perceived, that govern individual action. In the seventh degree of the Rite, the little black box of the Provost and Judge is where we hide, from others and ourselves, the "true" nature of our souls. Therefore the only truth often known is the truth of our own motivations. When we learn to see our motivations clearly, only then we can perceive and recognize the helpful or selfish motivations of others.

You cannot understand another's fear until you can recognize and set aside our own. You cannot see the truth until you set aside your own deceptions. Then the reality of any situation, set in the context of the actions directed by the emotions and motivations of the people involved, becomes clear. Then you have a truth.

How to see a Truth

This process is difficult at best. In this modern world of over stimulation how can a Mason find a reference point to even begin to see clearly? The quiet of nature is obliterated by the modern world. How can we learn from the lessons of nature and history if we are separated from them?

A good practical application of "seeing the truth" can be found in understanding the difference between amusement, information, knowledge, and wisdom. By learning how to recognize and separate the distractions of modern life from those things which are really useful to us we can *learn* to see the truth.

First recognize that much of the "information" we get is really only an attempt to distract our attention in order to receive something from us, specifically, our time and our money. Entertainers and merchants spend millions every hour to capture and hold your attention. It is not their mission to teach us or help us. They want us to give them our time and to buy their products. This does not mean that their motives are bad or that capitalism is evil. But in today's world of hyper-commercialism and instant communication, the flashing lights of entertainment and merchandising can blind us to enlightenment.

Amusement provides momentary entertainment or pleasant diversion but no useful or lasting information. This, in itself, is not a bad thing. A painting or a movie, a song or recording can sooth the mind and provide comfort and relieve stress. The issue is the sheer volume of amusement around us. Online videos, E-mail, social networking, and tweets on twitter can eat up much of our day and provide us with little or no real information.

Information as separate bits of data does not provide knowledge unless placed in comparative relation to other information to become knowledge. As with amusement the high volume of information we receive each day keeps us from analyzing it effectively. Another danger is that much of the information we will receive is not correct. Fantasies, illusions, distractions, and outright falsehoods abound. Even if something is not designed to deceive it can still misinform. Separate bits of information do not provide knowledge. Knowledge is dependent upon the individual's ability to both perceive *and* relate.

Knowledge is the recognition of how information relates to other information and how it affects people and things. Knowledge only comes after the individual has had time to think about information long enough to formulate a conclusion and experience enough to confirm what he has come to believe.

Wisdom is the ability to discern or judge what is true, right, or lasting, through the acquisition of knowledge, experience, understanding, common sense, and insight resulting in the ability to choose or act to consistently produce an optimum result. This is a life skill which is developed over time through study, experience, and contemplation.

In today's world we value amusement and information over knowledge. Wisdom is for the most part ignored and too often relegated to being the opinion of the old. If you can master your passions to move past amusement, sort through information, and calm yourself long enough to recognize knowledge you may find that you can see things for what they are and understand the motivations of others. In this ability you will see truth and find wisdom.

PART TWO:
TOOLS FOR MAKING A GOOD LIFE

CHAPTER FOUR: SOCIAL MESSAGES AND POLITICAL THEORY IN SCOTTISH RITE FREEMASONRY

Among the themes entwined in the degrees are the lessons of effective democratic and representative republic government which promote a free society. The applications of these lessons come in two interconnected themes. First is a social message which provides the intent and reasoning behind a particular idea. In many cases this is expressed in the form of a character or as the events within the story of the degree. Second is a political message which provides the methodology for implementing the idea expressed in the social message. Often, this is not expressly identified within the degree.

This is an important distinction. Masonry does not declare one form of freedom over another. It does not state that American democracy is better than French Liberty, the *form* of free government is less important than the *presence* of free government. The lessons apply as well to the British Parliament as it does to the American Congress.

As you study the degrees and find messages about social needs and political application use the framework described in this chapter to assist you in "finding the place" of the lesson within the degrees. These lessons deal with recognizing the working parts of a free and democratic society and the methods and institutions best suited to facilitate them. As you come across the lessons think about which parts address individual responsibilities and which parts address the functions of representative government.

As with other lessons within the ceremonies this social and political instruction is sometimes direct and at other times presented by parable, example, and allusion. Allusion is the most difficult to understand because an allusion is an idea which is represented or expressed as something else for the purpose of disguising the original intent. Remember that many of these ideas, like "one man one vote" and "representative government", were considered subversive and radical in the 17th and 18th century. The ideals that are normal and "common sense" today would have gotten men jailed or killed if openly expressed when kings still ruled.

Within the Blue Lodge degrees we find specific references to loyalty to government and obedience to the laws of the land. This concept of Social Contract addresses only the issue of submitting to just law for the purpose of maintaining good order within society. The Scottish Rite degrees explore beyond social contract to study the ideals that good laws should entail, and how they are implemented effectively within a democratic or representative government. Conversely, should some aspect of just law be repealed, or be found wanting, then the prudent Mason looks to why the system has changed and what can peaceably be done to direct government back on to a more noble course. Because "Just Law" is not intuitively known or universally acknowledged it must be studied, understood, promoted, and preserved by persons of benevolent and selfless motivation.

The social and political lessons are expressed in grouped ideas which are set incrementally within the degrees. Each series offers introductions, explanations, reiterations, and expansions on the tenets of a government of the people, by the people, and for the people.

Lodge of Perfection

The social and political lessons of the Lodge of Perfection are separated into three sections. The 4th through 6th degrees, Secret Master, Prefect Master, and Intimate Secretary, address the importance of the enlightened citizen. The 7th through 11th degree introduces the recognition of justice and the working parts of government. The 12th and 13th degrees, Master Architect and Royal Arch of Solomon, bring the lessons together with an explanation of the importance of strong leadership and a fundamental law to serve as a universal guide.

In the introduction to the Lodge of Perfection, the 4th, 5th, and 6th degrees, the message of Masonic Duty, Action now, and action with Zeal, respectively, is accompanied with the single political message of the importance of an enlightened citizenry where all men must take part in the formation and maintenance of the Social Contract. This simple message expresses the importance of interest and involvement in the political process. It is repeated three times to ensure the message sinks in because no other part of the free political process is possible without the enlightened citizen. As the Lodge of Perfection proceeds the social and political message turns to the recognition of justice in the 7th through 11th degrees.

In the 7th degree, Provost and Judge, Zebud is improperly asked to show favor as a judge. The lesson is that no prejudice should sway a court or tribunal. The best way to ensure that happens is to have an independent judiciary. This does two things. First it allows for judges to distance themselves from political issues and second, separates those who make the laws from those who apply them. This is an important part of the checks and balances that ensure our freedoms.

The 8th degree, Intendant of the Building, has King Solomon looking to the workmen to find new leadership for the completion of the Temple. He finds this leadership already within the work force. From this we learn that every laboring man is your brother and society requires all trades and skills. It is important to remember that strong economic order is based on capital and labor. This translates into the ideal that there must be a balance between those who rightfully profit from their ideas and those who labor to make those ideas a reality.

In the 9th degree, the Elu of the Nine search for the ruffians but when one of them is found there are only a few to bring him to justice: a Mason (the candidate) and Satolkin ben Hesed. The teaching point in this situation is even when we search in a group our actions are our own. The Mason strikes down the ruffian in self-defense when a noise reveals their attempt to capture him. With Satolkin ben Hesed's cry of "Vengeance!" at the ruffians' demise it is demonstrated that where the Mason seeks justice and order those in the grip of ignorance seek revenge. From this we can learn to recognize when men are in the grip of social despotism (Mob Rule) and that it is good to have leadership from wise men. This leadership can be provided in an upper house of legislation.

The 10th degree, Elu of the Fifteen, offers the second half of this lesson. As the second two ruffians are brought to answer for their crimes they are provided the opportunity to speak for themselves. This demonstrates that every man has a right to a voice, his own or a representative of his choosing. This describes a lower house of representatives.

The 11th degree, Elu of the Twelve, harkens back to the ideas on justice expressed in the 7th degree. Solomon's decision to dispatch 12 worthy men to oversee proper tax collection and to look after the interests of the people restores the worthiness of governance which was in the grip of tyranny expressed as unjust taxation. This tells us that civil order without justice is tyranny. The method described to maintain civil order is Trial by Jury. This may seem odd to our modern way of thinking but remember that until about three hundred years ago the King's representatives were the law and grievances would have gone before the very villains who were the cause of the dispute. This idea is revisited in the 21st degree, Prussian Knight.

In the conclusion of the Lodge of Perfection two vital themes come to light: leadership and consistency. In the 12th degree, Master Architect, leadership is expressed in Adoniram's promotion above his peers. Society requires leadership, vision, and mentorship. The recognition of a chief executive is imperative to a focused and forward moving society. But in contrast to the concept of a king, the vision provided by this Chief Executive is accountable to the will of the people.

This arrangement is articulated in a constitution or fundamental law which guides the leadership with ideals and functional rules to ensure the will of the people is not corrupted. In the 13th degree, The Royal Arch of Solomon, the finding of the Lost Word in Enoch's crypt shows that when order is lost, rules to govern should be found or established. This signifies that a society must have order and that the order should be clearly stated in a constitution or fundamental law. Also expressed is the lesson that when the modern fails, looking to what has worked in the past is prudent. Not to "go backwards" but rather to see what has worked well in the past and to use examples of historical success as a template for the future.

The 14th degree, Perfect Elu, is introspective and does not include any directly social or political messages. This is also true of the whole of the Chapter of Rose Croix which focuses on spiritual lessons and personal development.

Council of Kadosh

The degrees of the Council of Kadosh, being more focused on the instruction of knightly aspects of behavior and introduction to the esoteric Mysteries, spends more time on social messages than on political messages. Nonetheless, the few political messages that are found in the Council are really important and should not be overlooked. The 19th through the 24th degrees address Chivalric duties and codes of conduct. Within these lessons important social and political tenets are introduced to tutor the student of Masonry in the finer aspects of social contract. The 24th through the 27th degrees, Prince of the Tabernacle, Knight of the Brazen Serpent, Prince of Mercy, and Knight of the Sun, Prince Adept provide the wisdom required to guide and govern a society. The 28th degree, Knight Commander of the Temple instructs us in how to devote ourselves to the mastery of our own passions and the proper interpretations of what we see before us. The 29th and 30th degrees, Knight of Saint Andrew and Knight Kadosh speak directly to those aspects of freedom which are imperative to the success of a free society.

The 19th degree, Grand Pontiff, and 20th degree, Master of the Mystic Lodge, sets the stage very well with the messages that leaders must build for the future, just as those who came before us built for us; and the importance of recognizing that societies are influenced by multiple motivations and even more by traditions. We should therefore look to multiple traditions for guidance on how to make a free and just society. Specifically, political systems should be based on, and support, the ideals of the noblest aspects of past and current civilizations. By learning from the many we strengthen the one. You may recognize this lesson in the Latin phrase "E Pluribus Unum" From many, one.

In the 21st degree, Prussian Knight, we witness the gross misuse of power by a tribunal member. This reinforces the lesson that any authority used to silence the voice of the people is unjust and stands to represent the importance, and political necessity, of Freedom of the Press in the protection of liberty. This is a refined message from the one addressed in the 7th degree, the importance of being an impartial judge.

The 22nd degree, Knight of the Royal Axe, teaches that society requires the full spectrum of labor from grave digger to architect and emphasizes the equality of all men. To facilitate that tenet of freedom Masonry teaches that no class system should be established or allowed to develop which subjugate free men within any law or political system.

In the 23rd degree, Chief of the Tabernacle, we find the anchor point for all that has come before and all that will come after in relation to social and political messages. This degree is a preparation for the candidate to ready himself to receive the Mysteries and it offers a point that will seem in later degrees to be a contradiction. The first point is the importance of the belief in Deity within a society. Belief in Deity provides the moral compass for the people. No matter if there is only one kind of house of worship or many different ones, the lack of any houses of worship will doom a society to failure. This manifests politically within the law as an agreement among the citizenry on how they will live together as a society. This establishes the social contract within the citizenry.

This is the reason the Mystery degrees are expressed with prominence. The 24th through the 27th degrees, Prince of the Tabernacle, Knight of the Brazen Serpent, Prince of Mercy, and Knight of the Sun, Prince Adept provide this imperative message in respect to social and political justice. In order for us to be able to search for Deity as individuals we must include Deity as part of society. Also expressed here is the belief that within all cultures and religions there are similarities; truths that have stood the test of time. The study of these similarities will reveal those things that wise men have accepted as true for thousands of years.

The 27th degree, Knight of the Sun, Prince Adept, and seems almost completely introspective but it is not. It specifically addresses how we deal with the belief systems of people and how we plan to conduct ourselves in the presence of others as a global citizen. As masters of our passions and leaders of our communities we are instructed to see ourselves and to comprehend the past. The Prince Adept is instructed to understand that history repeats itself and to learn from a community's past to see its future.

In the 28th Degree, The Knight Commander of the Temple must be man enough to admit his errors and amend them, and also be man enough to peacefully reconcile differences with his brother. The Knight's vigil is not a test of physical strength but of a man's true strength, his moral resolution and fortitude.

In the 29th Degree, as a Knight of Saint Andrew, we bring together the aspects of knighthood. In recognizing knighthood, not as an individual philosophy but as a collective strength we can look to our peers, identify the true defenders of freedom, and support them. Politically this support includes laws that promote and protect Freedom of Ideas and Thought was well as Freedom of Speech.

The Knight Kadosh, 30th degree, contains the last unifying messages of social and political mechanism. First is to believe in being a loyal and peaceable citizen and that all citizens should be loyal to the rightful government and strive to obey the laws thereof. Second, that there should be a separation of church and state. This is the contradiction identified earlier. The moral compass provided by reverence of Deity is imperative to the strength of a nation but no one aspect of reverence, or one belief system, should ever be the mechanism with which that moral compass is established for all. This lesson is also centrally reinforced in the 27th degree.

You may well recognize the use of the words Strength and Establishment. These are the definitions for the names of the pillars Jachin and Boaz. Supported above the strength of Deity and the establishment of governance is the mantel (stability) of a nation. The visualization of the mantel stone supported by two pillars is powerful and revered from antiquity. It is unfortunate that historic examples of a living man having the authority to speak as, or for, God, who also served in the role of a national leader, has rendered such a long and terrible litany of universally catastrophic failures. This is not to say they did not establish themselves and thrive. The example of Egypt alone is enough to exemplify the point. What the combination of church and state has never provided is government by the consent of the governed, with equal treatment for all.

Consistory

The Consistory provides something slightly different than the social and political messages in the other degrees. Where the 4th though the 30th degrees describe what good government looks like and what it provides to the people, the Consistory speaks to our relationship with government and what end state government should provide.

The 31st degree, Inspector Inquisitor, addresses the issue of judgment and justice. By definition "justice" is God's perfect understanding and infallible balance between mercy and condemnation. The purpose of Justice is to reward or punish according to God's will. "Law" is man's attempt to mirror God's justice. The wise understand that law is not perfect and that its purpose is solely to maintain order within society. The social contract of law is the tool society uses to protect itself from individual acts of retribution and to ensure the people that their grievances will be addressed by the whole for the betterment of the whole. Retribution, or "Vengeance", is an illusion within the mind of man that his actions can dispense God's perfect justice. It is an emotional desire to harm another person for the purpose of indulging an individual desire to feel satisfaction by the pain, discomfort, or embarrassment of another who has committed a real or perceived transgression. It is important for a Mason to understand that man's law provides order, not justice.

In the 32nd degree, Master of the Royal Secret, there is a specific articulation of the true freedoms which government should provide. Every man should have the right to live as he sees fit as long as he does not infringe on the rights of others. Included in this is the freedom to think, learn, and openly discuss ideas; freedom to worship Deity as he sees fit without the pressure of religious tyranny; freedom from tyranny in the form of the right to vote on those issues that affect him and to speak openly about any issue with which he may take exception; and most importantly, the right to defend himself, his family, his property, and his Liberty. This is the reason the camp is assembled on the field. This is the reason men take up arms. This is the reason men seek peace through learning, fraternity, worship, and the mastery of their passions.

Conclusion

These are the social and political messages laid out within the degrees of Scottish Rite Masonry in the Southern Jurisdiction. These lessons reflect a political ideal which was lost in the fall of Greece, and then again with the fall of Rome. As the world shrugged off the dark ages these ideas took root again. It was not until the 1500's that men could discuss these ideas openly and it was another 200 years until they came to fruition, and then only by revolution was tyranny set aside (most certainly not defeated). What seems normal and right today was wild heresy and treason not too long ago. The lessons in the degrees are important and should be studied.

The descriptions provided in this chapter are by no means complete and further study is warranted in all of the degrees in order for the messages identified therein to be fully understood in context with the other related lessons included in the degrees.

CHAPTER FIVE: ANSWERS TO QUESTIONS ABOUT MASONIC SECRECY, CONSPIRACY, MOTIVATION, AND CONTROL.

What is the purpose of secrecy in Masonry?

The purpose of secrecy in Masonry is to teach men how to know something without revealing what they know: to teach an honest man how to know a thing and never speak of it. This is different from teaching a man the art of deception. To tell a lie is not consistent with Masonic philosophy and there is no Masonic instruction which teach a man how to lie. What Masons do learn is how to trust another individual and how to keep a confidence. They also learn how to, and when to, conceal their thoughts, beliefs, and associations. Although this may seem nefarious to those outside of Masonry it is a very real necessity for the preservation of those things held in reverence by Masonry. Masonic secrecy is not conspiratorial or aggressive but rather protective and defensive.

If Masonry were a secret then Lodges would not be listed in the phone book. The things we hold dear; faith, hope, charity, and love of Deity are not secrets. So if who we are and what we care for are not secret, then why do we practice secrecy? I submit to you that the purpose of Masonic secrecy is not to preserve the institution of Masonry but rather the things Masonry holds in reverence: spiritual, social, and political liberty.

Why is secrecy an integral part of Masonic teachings?

It is a well-known lesson of history that people learn from their societies; from their parents, friends, teachers, and churches. They learn especially from their culture and their country. We will do what is ingrained in us from training, life experience, or habit. For this reason Masonry teaches, in constant and subtle ways, the methods of knowing a thing without speaking of it. It teaches men how to communicate in symbols, pictures, and codes. Some secrets are ceremonial. Masons recognize other Masons by subtle signs, grips, words, and tokens. These are the universal methods used by Masons to recognize each other worldwide.

It is important to recognize, however, that it is not the lessons of Masonry that are secret. The degrees and ceremonies have all been revealed in books and on the Internet. The secrets are the methods Masons use to recognize each other as fraternal brothers, these are the secrets that are most often kept, but even these can be found by those who apply themselves. So if it is not the information we are keeping secret then, why do we practice secrecy?

Who would Masons need to hide these things from?

Some ideas of fraternal secrecy are historical. Remember that in the beginning of Masonry concepts like "one man one vote" and "equality of man" were not acceptable to the ruling classes. Men who spoke or acted upon the ideals of liberty, which are taken for granted in a free society as "rights", were imprisoned, their lands and holdings taken, their families lost. Even today there are parts of the world where repressive governments still hold power over the people. In these places, where Masonry is growing, free thinking men must hide their activities or risk the full weight of repression just as it was in much of central Europe in the 1700's.

Within living memory despots and tyrants have been bent on world domination and in every case their horrid plans began within their own homelands. Starting small, they used the fear and ignorance of the people to advantage and spoke of dangers which required the suspension of liberty for the protection of what was "good and right". First taking rights from those who could not object, and then from those who had watched the gradual degradation of freedom until there was no one left to object, when all those who might object would be labeled as criminal thinkers.

This lesson of history cannot be ignored and freedom loving men must prepare for, and defend against, the erosion of liberty and the social and political situations that lead to tyrannical government and spiritual despotism. This is often secret work. But this in no way implies that Masons are disloyal to their respective governments, against religion, or that they want to "take over". What it does mean is that the best way to preserve freedom and stability is to know what good government and freedom of religion look like, and how to recognize the degradation of these worthy institutions early in the process, in order to preserve them. Masons hide their actions from those who seek to enslave and control the people. This is the secret nature of our civic work.

Is there really a Masonic conspiracy and what is its goal?

Masonry does not seek to control men but to educate and free them. The Masonic conspiracy is reserved for those times when the rights of free men are denied. Those who fear Masonry are those who would deny men their freedom. Those who wish to destroy Masonry are those who want no competition when they attempt to impose their will through the promotion of ignorance and superstition by means of fear, coercion, intimidation, or brute force.

The goal of Masonry is to educate a host of men who are trained in the philosophies and mechanisms of free society. Who can, when the situation requires, use the methods of secrecy, and are prepared and willing to act in freedoms defense. Nothing is more intimidating to a despot than the thought of free and educated men who are unified in their resolution and willing to act. Masons are a population of prepared, practiced, and willing minds ready to oppose tyranny. Masonry was created, in part, as a movement to promote and preserve the tenets of liberty.

This does not mean that Masons are a secret army. Despite their association with the Templar armies of the past, modern Masons are not particularly well organized outside of their scholastic endeavors and are certainly not unified in any military efforts. Masonic "camps" are symbolic, their "ranks" are ceremonial, and there is no martial training of any kind. What they are is very consistent in the teaching of historically important philosophies. The strength of Masonry comes from cumulative efforts of individual members acting for the common good.

Who controls the Masons?

As a group Masons are an organization of men who promote enlightenment and who regulate themselves by following the lessons of time honored wisdom. Although there is a definite and well established hierarchy of leadership within Masonry, this leadership governs only by the consent of the membership. Because Masonry is a fraternal organization there is no binding obligation on any man other than what his constitution will bear.

Blue Lodge Masonry around the world is divided into Grand Jurisdictions. In the United States, a Grand Jurisdiction is generally a State or Territory. The Scottish Rite is divided into the Northern Jurisdiction of 15 northeastern states, situated east of the Mississippi and north of the rivers of Ohio, and the Southern Jurisdiction which consists of the remainder of the United States and Orients from around the globe. Each jurisdiction is governed by its own Supreme Council. A state or "Orient" in the Scottish Rite is divided into "Valleys" or areas served by a Scottish Rite Temple.

A Mason is never under any obligation to follow an instruction which causes him to set aside his duty to God, Family, or Country. Should a Mason act in a manner seriously contrary to the tenets of known wisdom, detrimental to society, or criminal, he is separated from the Masons. There is an undeniably full and sensationalized history of men who have joined Masonry in an attempt to advance themselves and their private agendas. In most cases, with time, these men show their true colors, are found out, and are removed from the lodge. When this happens the actions of the wayward individual are sometimes reported as the actions of the Masons as a whole.

At other times men emulate the ceremonies of Masonry. In some cases they seek to imitate the pageantry or laudable tenets of Masonry. Some others have no true understanding of Masonry or what it stands for but attempt to add a façade of nobility or mystery to their nefarious causes. The currently active Ku Klux Klan is an infamous example of this. The actions of these imitators and imposters are sometime attributed to Masonry and the silence of Masons does not assist in dispelling these attributions, but in the end it is the true and positive aspects of Masonry which sustain it, and allow it to withstand the insincerities of ruffians, impostors, and imitators.

Is Masonry a religion?

Freemasonry is most definitely not a religion. Granted, it does involve the study of philosophy and theology which makes it easy to see why some may mistake the philosophies and life guidance found within Freemasonry as religion, but upon closer inspection one finds that Freemasonry does not meet the definitions required of a religion. Although philosophy and religion share curtain similarities like "search for truth" and "life guidance" it is important to make note of some significant differences.

Philosophy is the study of ideas. No philosophy can claim correctness in any way other than through the test of time. In order to continue to be held as true an idea or philosophy must be repeatedly tested and found valid over an extended period of human experience. No philosophy can assure forgiveness of sins or atonement in the eyes of God. Finally, although philosophy argues its points of correctness in the pursuit of truth, philosophy does not convert for the purpose of saving ones soul. In order to define the differences between philosophy and religion more clearly a definition of religion should be examined.

Religions are generally defined by three things. First, they offer a plan of salvation which becomes a system of belief in an eternal life based on faith and achieved through a prescribed path or discipline. This is theology. Religions then seek adherents to follow the elements of faith prescribed. Second, religions believe eternal bliss requires atonement of the human condition, and therefore offer methods of redemption for past sins and purification of the soul. Finally, religions offer atonement and profess to cleanse souls for the purpose of salvation. There are examples of religions which do not seek converts, as in the case of Zoroastrianism and conservative Orthodox Judaism. These are still, quite correctly, considered religions. On the negative side, some religions tend to reject other belief systems and dissuade all study of views other than their own. It is because Masonry meets none of these criteria that it cannot be considered a religion. An examination of each criteria will show this to be true.

Freemasonry studies the philosophies of past civilizations, including their religions, but does not claim any one to be "the truth" over all others. Freemasons believe that there is truth to be found in every religion and that there are universal truths that can lead a man to enlightenment. Additionally, Masonry teaches that diligent study, contemplation and application of those concepts found universally in all religions is essential to harmony in the world. The philosophies of Freemasonry do not promise atonement, forgiveness, or spiritual salvation; but that the study of the Truth can allow a man to better understand Divinity, however he may personally perceive the nature of God. Finally, and very importantly, Freemasonry does not recruit or "convert" anyone to its philosophies. To join the Masons a man must seek out the Masons and must ask to join. "Ask one to be one." This motto of the Freemason's is of paramount importance when discussing the idea of Freemasonry as a religion. Masonry does not convert a man to, or draw a man away from, any one religion. It is not a replacement for religion and does not seek men for the purpose of saving their souls. Many men have joined Masonry in the misguided hope of finding a Masonic religion only to be disappointed in this illusion.

An impassioned argument made against Masonry is that it "diverts" the efforts of men away from their respective religions. This is not true. What it does is invite men to study the nature of divinity and to think independently about the nature of man's relationship with God. These arguments that men are "diverted" from God by Masonry are only made by religious leaders and their supporters who are invested, either knowingly or by ignorance, in spiritual despotism and who fear having their demands for compliance scrutinized by free thinking men; or they are not secure in the rightness of their faith and do not want it to be too closely scrutinized. There is no time or circumstance when the study of theology and philosophy are detrimental to a true reverence of Deity.

PART THREE:
GOALS OF THE JOURNEY

CHAPTER SIX: THE FIVE VOWS

The Five Vows of the 32nd degree address those things we promise to do in the service of our communities and our fellow man. The vows speak directly to our actions in the preservation of liberty through making ourselves better citizens, promoting and protecting the rights of others, and encouraging others to recognize and act in the preservation of their own freedoms. The Five Vows state that by example and through our actions we will actively work against tyranny, superstition, despotism, and ignorance.

Note: The vows included here in italics are not the exact vows from the degree. They are paraphrased for the specific purpose of not putting ritual text into print. These versions effectively express the general intent of the vows but the real vows should be studied and reflected upon. The verbatim vows are available in the 32nd degree ceremony script, copies of which can be found in every Valley.

THE FIRST VOW

I promise that I will do what I can to help other men be wiser and better. That I will continue my efforts to better myself and attend meetings of the Masonic organizations of which I am a member. I will read, with an open mind, Masonic books designed to enlighten the willing, and I promise to be a faithful Soldier of the Light.

A Soldier of the Light is not a light giver. He must be a light bearer because no man can compel the heart of another. Light must be found by each individual. Only by his own example can a Soldier of Light awaken the desire of emulation in another. Not a faint imitation but a true desire to seek the wisdom he sees within a man who is the master of his own being.

THE SECOND VOW

I promise not to misuse any power or position I may hold. I will not allow, if it is within my power to prevent, any man to take advantage of another and I will promote freedom of thought and speech as well as the right to vote for all men. I will be my own master in action and intellect, and let no other tell me what to think or do beyond proper civil law. I promise to be a Soldier of Liberty.

Liberty requires unending effort and constant vigilance. The Soldier of Liberty never indulges in the ease of allowing another to speak for him, nor with arrogance, believes he has the authority to speak for another without due consent. He will evoke, when appropriate, the power of his own voice, for to remain silent is to abdicate one's freedom. Remembering always that liberty dies by slim degrees and slips away when not kept under a watchful eye.

THE THIRD VOW

I promise I will actively work against any spiritual oppression of the will or mind of any man. I will deny the attempts of any religion to use force, threat, or superstition to compel men to submit to dogmatic demands. When I can, I will replace superstition with truth, and will shame the hateful and unthinking by exposing them to thoughtful scrutiny. I promise to be a Soldier of Freedom of Religion.

The Soldier of Freedom of Religion remembers that every man has the right to live his life as he sees fit, as long as he does not infringe upon the rights of others. When any man claims to speak with the authority of Deity he is surely a false prophet. This is the favorite tool of spiritual tyranny. The Soldier of Freedom of Religion knows not to directly confront spiritual tyranny, for to do so only emboldens the charlatan with the attention he desires. Instead, the Soldier of Freedom of Religion speaks the truth in a calm and quiet voice, appealing to the calm reason of men and dispelling the dark thoughts invoked by fear mongers.

THE FOURTH VOW

I promise to do what I can to stop unworthy men from coming to positions of authority. I will encourage men to act and think for themselves. I promise to be a Soldier of the People.

A Soldier of the People reminds his fellows that anything too good to be true is most likely false. Those who promise to do for others those things others should do for themselves steal independence. He who promises to make another man's life easier steals that man's ability to live free. Do not confuse this trait with those who serve honorably in capacities of true human service; the Doctor, the Soldier, the Caregiver, or the skilled Craftsman and Artisan. As the vow clearly states, it is the crafty, the unfit, and the incompetent who must be guarded against.

THE FIFTH VOW

I promise to do those things which Masonic teachings have asked me to do; to attend meetings when I can and assist even when I cannot attend. I will keep the goals of Masonry in mind at all times and will act to the advancement of those goals. I promise to be a Soldier of the Scottish Rite. I will say what I mean; mean what I say, live honorably, and make my actions a positive tribute to the Masons who came before me.

This is not a promise to attend meetings and pay dues. This speaks directly to your participation in the efforts of the respective Bodies of Scottish Rite Masonry and betterment of yourself through a life long association with honorable fellows. To stand with your peers as a Soldier of the Scottish Rite. For even as a single drop of sea water is an ocean in itself, when combined with its fellows it joins into the crashing seas that bring life to the world and shape the continents.

CHAPTER SEVEN: THE CAMP

The Camp is a representation of the studies and personal journey each Mason is encouraged to make as a Master of the Royal Secret. The shapes and the objects (or lack of objects) are depictions of areas of study and the progressive goals achievable through those areas of study. Although Masonry does not teach esoteric lessons there are symbols within the Camp which can point a Mason to areas of esoteric study which will be required for him to undertake to complete his journey.

The Camp is divided into five sections. The nonagon is symbolic of the course of study required for the prerequisite broadening of the man. This is done through the study of the aspects of the heptagon, representing the physical aspects of the seven "planets" or Lesser Mysteries. Once these are mastered the candidate progresses to the Pentagon which symbolizes that man should subject his elemental or lower nature to the influences of the Divine Spirit through the study of the Greater Mysteries. Through this course of study the Mason transforms through the spiritual alchemy represented in the Triangle, finally passing to the circle which represents Deity. Here the Mason has the opportunity to discover his relationship with Deity and even the divine nature within himself. It is vital to understand that because Scottish Rite Masonry is not a formal Mystery School this diagram is only representative of the process. The Master of the Royal Secret has been shown the path but not taken completely through the process. He has the tools, the introduction, and the described path, but the remaining journey is completely incumbent upon his own desire, true and successful progression, and his spiritual constitution.

Nonagon: Starting from the outside there is the Nonagon with its nine sides. The nonagon is described in the fourth degree as a base to build upon. The tents of the nonagon include the degrees of the Blue lodge, the Lodge of Perfection, and the Chapter of Rose Croix. Reflection upon the degrees represented under the respective standards is instructional. These can be found in the ceremony script of the 32nd degree and a reading of the descriptions of the standards will help you understand their meaning.

Heptagon: A clue to the learning goals of these degrees is found in the barrier to progression to the tents of the higher degrees. For this reason the next shape seen is the seven sided heptagon which is representative of the seven "planets", the liberal arts, the Nine Great Truths of Masonry and the Lesser Mysteries, which make up the myriad lessons in these developmental degrees. In the latter degrees of this progression, The Master Architect, the candidate is introduced to the tools of physical drafting used in the creation of shapes and angles. His mastery of these physical aspects denotes the prerequisite broadening of the man. The heptagon having been mastered, or passed, the candidate advances to the pennants found on the five sided pentagon.

Pentagon: Upon the pentagon are the pennons of degrees which represent the training of a Knight aspirant which culminates in the declaration of the candidate as a Knight of the Sun, Prince Adept. In the 27th degree there are a large number of symbolic designs including the circle, the vesica pisces, the creation of a triangle, the pentagram, the Vitruvian man, the 90 Degree angle, Pie (3.1415), the heptagram, the Pythagorean tetractys, the use of the Tetractys in forming triangles, the Tetractys forming the Seal of Solomon and High Priest's Jewel, the Tetractys forming a cube, and the Tetractys forming a Tetragrammaton. Only a Mason well versed in the physical aspects of these procedures will be able to understand the transformative and spiritual aspects of these symbols.

Triangle: Within the triangle of the Camp are the images of a Black Raven, a White Dove, and a Red Phoenix. These symbols are a specific reference to the stages of progression within the process of spiritual alchemy.[21] As the Mason passes the triangle through the completion of the process he comes into the circle, the symbol of one, and is able to come face to face with Deity and the divine aspects of himself.

Note: Within the triangle the candidate is also reintroduced to the elements mentioned in the Blue Lodge degrees. Now much more meaningful; chalk, charcoal, and clay now denote spiritual alchemy and the process is hinted at when the REBIS is shown to the candidate. The Raven, Dove, and Phoenix are specific clues to the requirements of passage. The symbols of the REBIS now lay out a path of enlightenment which is revealed to the Master of the Royal Secret. The path is shown; the Mason must make the journey ahead on his own. Study here the phrases of "incomparable treasure" and "inner light" as mentioned in the 32nd degree. They are clues for those who would seek the secret of the REBIS. The REBIS is the key to moving from the Pentagon through the Triangle to the circle. This is not a trip every Mason will attempt and of those who attempt it only a few will complete the transmutation.

Circle: Here is found the cross of Saint Andrew, but it is different than you have seen it before. Now at its center is the tent of the Grand Commander and at the end of each arm is a tent for the four Inspectors General, who each hold the authority of a Marshal. Although this is where the Grand Commander and his Marshals reside, look to the symbol for the meaning. Why is the Grand Commander's tent over the point of the circumpunct? The two V shapes meeting in the middle: As it is above so it is below. Go back and review the Worm Ouroboros and the Great Seal of Solomon from the 27th degree. Nothing in this book will truly explain what they really mean. If you make the journey you may discover the truth for yourself.

There is a reason for the great care and significant amount of time dedicated to the descriptions of the lessons of the tents and pennons during the conduct of the Master of the Royal Secret degree. This is because these lessons address the building of the man. There is also a reason why the description ends before you arrive at the triangle. You must make this part of the journey yourself.

The journey is extremely difficult, time consuming, and, some say, impossible without the assistance of a learned mentor from a School of Mystery. In the past, great civic leaders and military generals trained with the Mystery Schools and progressed past the heptagon to the pentagon but no further due to the time requirements demanded of complete self actualization.

We as men in the modern world are most likely never going to encounter a true Mystery School but the process is not completely denied to us. The requirements are provided and the pitfalls are forewarned so that we may, by our own endeavors, seek that light which is not hidden, but only secret by being unseen. Understand that the learning process provided in Scottish Rite Masonry is a life's work and, more importantly, that a good man, who walks any part of this path, will in fact benefit from it, no matter how far his constitution or situation allows him to proceed.

This is the message and the secret of the Camp.

CHAPTER EIGHT: THE DIFFERENCE BETWEEN MASONRY AND MYSTERY SCHOOLS

The Mysteries are an important part of Masonic teaching and should be addressed with serious study by all Masons. That being said, the Greater Mysteries are not for everybody. One of the main tenets of the Mystery Schools, as well as Masonry, is that men progress only as far as their constitution allows and that very few men reach the highest levels of "awareness". In many cases men who were groomed for political and military leadership were trained in the Lesser Mysteries to provide a strong base for their life's work and then received limited introduction to the Greater Mysteries because the time required and stress involved in the higher pursuits would draw them away from the duties of their positions. The duties and demands of modern life seem to have an equally limiting effect on Masons today.

Scottish Rite Masonry is not a Mystery School. Although it introduces the concepts and teaching points to important lessons of the Lesser Mysteries they are not specifically taught but rather alluded to in the degrees. The candidate is encouraged to study and learn more on their own. Phrases like, "we learn from ancient writings" and "our study of geometry" indicate that our knowledge of the Lesser Mysteries comes from our own endeavors after the presentation of the degrees. This in no way limits a Mason from completing the Mystical journey on his own accord. Having the assistance of persons who have studied the Mysteries is very helpful but not a requirement for success in discovering oneself.

A Mystery School is a university of the soul, a school for the study of the mysteries of the inner nature of man and the Divine lessons found in nature. By understanding these mysteries, the student perceives his intimate relationship with divinity, and strives through self-discipline and devotion to become at one with his inner spirit which is a part of Divinity. Although many of these aspects are mentioned and even revealed in the Scottish Rite Degrees they are not directly imparted in the same manner they would be in a formal Mystery School.

In the Lesser Mysteries many branches of the arts and sciences were taught as a method of introducing the initiate to the realities of the natural world, notably geography, astronomy, chemistry, physiology, psychology, geology, meteorology, as well as music, which is described as the "most divine and *spiritual* of arts".[22] It is important to differentiate between these subjects being taught as subjects of physical science and these same subjects being taught as esoteric lessons. In physical science the focus of study is on the effects of nature, whereas in the esoteric schools these same subjects are studied as causal.

These Lesser Mysteries are introduced throughout all 32 degrees beginning with the Entered Apprentice. The importance of the message of "look for these things" is imperative and not to be taken lightly or seen as a weakness in the lessons of Masonic degrees. No other organization makes as strong or complete of an introduction to the Mysteries as Masonry without demanding significant obligations of the initiate. You will note that in the degrees we refer to Candidates and Aspirants, never to Initiates. The distinction is exact and purposeful.

This does not lessen the importance of the lessons in Masonry. There are vital clues to the Mysteries scattered like gems throughout the degrees. Some of the introductions impart knowledge of significance to the Mystery Degrees. The pillars of Wisdom, Strength, and Beauty in conjunction with the tenets of Masonry are as strong of an introduction to the Kabbalistic tree of life as can be found anywhere. The specific notations of Pythagorean mathematics are a direct indication of items of great importance to the study of the Lesser Mysteries. The admonishments to the Candidate to pursue these studies with vigor are not idle suggestions. They are meant to be followed with diligence, reverence and reason.

The Greater Mysteries are specifically not taught in Freemasonry, only some of the religions that the Greater Mysteries are based. The Mystery Schools themselves often have seven degrees in which the first four degrees are preparation for the last three.[23] The first four degrees generally strengthen and fortify the mind through study and contemplation in order for the man to be able to withstand the stresses of the three higher degrees. The initiate meets and conquers death in some real and life threatening way in order to "experience the reality", and if successful he moves on to the higher degrees. In the higher degrees the initiate sets his ego aside, perceives the essence of Deity, and eventually becomes one with this essence.

These degrees generally flow in line with teachings about the seven aspects, or substance principles, of the human condition. They are separated into four earthly and three spiritual elements. The lower four consist of elements which translate roughly to worldly desire, life spark, astral body, and physical body. The higher three consist of spirit (consciousness), soul (intellect), and mind (ego).

Some of these same elements are found in Scottish Rite Degrees. A good example of this is found in the 30th degree where the candidate encounters the specter of a past candidate who was unable to master his fear of death and so failed, falling victim to his fear. The specter gives grave warning and implores the candidate to flee for his life but the candidate is resolved to continue, masters his fear of death, and finds himself vindicated and accepted by the Frank Judges, the arbiters of his life. This degree shares similar aspects reportedly found within the fourth degree of the Mysteries but the difference is that in the Mystery schools the Initiate faces a much greater real or perceived mortal danger.

Should a Mason decide to pursue initiation or receive an invitation into one of the Mystery Schools he would find himself adequately introduced to the knowledge required of an Initiate and with further guided study may well advance successfully.

PART FOUR:
STUDY NOTES

The Great Seal of Solomon

CHAPTER NINE: NOTES ON SYMBOLS

The purpose of studying symbols is to use them as clues to learn the *Lessons of Nature.* Comprehension of the lessons of nature will lead a Masonic student to understanding things that are real in nature and true in the motivations of men.

Symbols must be addressed with care as they are designed to conceal as well as convey. Over time a symbol can take on a meaning conceptually beyond, unrelated to, or even opposite from its original meaning. The symbol itself can offer a clue to its original meaning. Some symbols may look like a letter from a written language and are designed to hide their origins. Others are pictographic or representative of motion which was intended to be recognized and understood by persons with the training or ability to do so. The older symbols tend to be of this latter nature as they represented physical things or practical knowledge.

Examples of physical things can be found in the symbols of the Zodiac. Some of these symbols are easily recognizable to us today like the stylized horns of the ram representing Aries and the crossed arrow for Sagittarius. Others have become more stylized with time like the circle and hook representing a lion's head for Leo and the two pillars representing the twins of Gemini. In Gemini's case it may be an example of a lost reference. We know the "twin" sign stands for two of something but we have lost the original reference. The two pillars may well have represented the two pillars of Upper and Lower Egypt. If you are not familiar with this reference the symbol loses, or changes, its representative context.

Two examples of symbols representing practical knowledge are symbols related to mathematics and observation of motion. For mathematics, the symbol for Pisces (two outward facing half circles joined with a short line at their mid point) is supposed to represent a fish. When a pair of circles (or half circles) are overlapped at their respective midpoints, the likeness of a fish appears. This was an important lesson in relative scale to early mathematicians as the dimensions of the "fish" from side to side and mouth to tail was always a ratio of 153:265 (in whole numbers) regardless of the size of the two equal circles. To the initiated this was easily recognizable as the Vesica Pisces, but a person untrained in mathematics would not understand the fish reference nor comprehend the mathematics it represented. For motion, the crescent of the moon is an easily recognized and commonly used symbol. The motion of the shadow across the surface of the moon has been immediately recognizable to both trained and untrained people throughout history.

This may seem obvious and simple but other motion symbols have been less recognizable and more problematic. There is a symbol which once represented knowledge, then forbidden knowledge, and eventually was twisted into a sign of evil. For those who studied the motion of the "planets" visible to the naked eye in ancient times, (Sun, Moon, Venus, Mars, Mercury, Jupiter, and Saturn) there was a wealth of information to be found. Sometimes this knowledge threatened the power of politics and religion. The pentagram was originally a representation of the movement of the planet Venus which, over an eight year time frame, aligns between the earth and the sun five times, moving 3/5 of the orbit of the earth between each alignment, called a synod. When you draw a star by crossing five equal lines returning to the start point you will find two things: first, you can draw a perfect circle by following the points of the star, and second, you have just accurately diagramed the synod sequence of earth's alignments with Venus.

This pattern has been known for thousands of years and was considered a secret of the most learned and wise. Even the biblical figure of Solomon was thought to have used a symbol of a five pointed star with the pentagon at its center. It has been speculated that those who understood the celestial origin of this symbol may well have also understood important lessons of nature. They may have known that the earth moved around the sun and could predict the movements of the planets. This knowledge eventually came into conflict with those political and religious powers that chose to rule through fear and superstition. It is important to remember that in ancient times there was little difference between religion and politics, high priests and kings moved in the same courts of power and governance. Soon the pentagram began to be seen as a symbol of those who were enemies of the ruling powers and in time some political and religious rulers, beginning far before the Christians, literally turned the sign of the elegant and ever present movement of the second planet into a mark of evil, damnation, selfishness, and destruction; the inverted pentacle.

The pentagram in a circle, or pentacle, is a commonly misused sign. It is turned upside down to misrepresent, or reverse, its meaning. In simplistic terms this is the story of how a symbol's meaning is changed. In the Middle-Ages the church identified and persecuted people who understood science as heretics. The symbols these learned men used, like the pentagram representing the movement of Venus, were decried by the church as "proof" of anti-church or evil ways. Eventually those who purposely aligned themselves away from the church took the symbol once used by learned men and literally turned it to their own uses with no regard for the original meaning of the symbol. It is not uncommon for symbols to be slightly altered and attribute new meanings regardless of the original lesson of nature represented by the symbol. This does nothing more than add distance between the symbol and the truth it originally represented.

As a Mason you should recognize the aspects of Fanaticism and Despotism at work here by cruel and selfish people who wish to spread fear and promote superstition. This diversion from the truth is the very thing we work against as bridge builders and bearers of light.

On a less sinister, but equally misguiding, note some symbols take on a greater meaning than they originally represented. The symbol of life from ancient Egypt was the Ankh, a cross with a loop over the cross bar. From time in memorial the Ankh has stood for life, fertility, and growth. There is a reason for this. In Samaria and Egypt, where the rain is too infrequent to sustain agricultural plant life, the annual floods were vital to the growth of food. This was true between the rivers Tigris and Euphrates as well as along the Nile.

It was important to get just the right amount of flooding. Too little and not enough rich silt would be left behind, too much and people died in the floods, their homes destroyed. To keep track of just how much flooding was "just right" a stick was placed in the ground with a bar tied across it to mark the high water mark which experience had identified as just the right amount of flooding. Later a hoop was added so priests could gauge when the floods would crest and subside by the rising of the sun or particular stars within the hoop when viewed from a certain angle. The Ankh was the representation of the "river stick" and in time the symbol took on the meaning of the information it provided: life and growth.

This is important as people will mistakenly empower the symbol with the attributes of what it represents. The Egyptians knew the "river stick" was important and what it revealed to them could mean life or death. In time the symbol was attributed with the power of life it represented. People began to think the symbol itself held the power of life. This can be seen today with the symbol of Christ. The crucifix currently represents the love and power of God but it is not magical or other worldly on its own. There are no magic symbols, only the powers in nature or in Divinity those symbols represent.

A reading of the 25th Degree in Albert Pike's *Morals and Dogma* is very relevant here and this short excerpt puts into perspective the importance of seeing symbols for their original stated purpose.

Thus, naturally and necessarily, time was divided, first into days, and then into moons or months, and years; and with these divisions and the movements of the Heavenly bodies that marked them, were associated and connected all men's physical enjoyments and privations. Wholly agricultural, and in their frail habitations greatly at the mercy of the elements and the changing seasons, the primitive people of the Orient were most deeply interested in the recurrence of the periodical phenomena presented by the two great luminaries of Heaven, on whose regularity all their prosperity depended.

And the attentive observer soon noticed that the smaller lights of Heaven were, apparently, even more regular than the Sun and Moon, and foretold with unerring certainty, by their risings and settings, the periods of recurrence of the different phenomena and seasons on which the physical well-being of all men depended. They soon felt the necessity of distinguishing the individual stars, or groups of stars, and giving them names, that they might understand each other, when referring to and designating them. Necessity produced designations at once natural and artificial. Observing that, in the circle of the year, the renewal and periodical appearance of the productions of the earth were constantly associated, not only with the courses of the Sun, but also with the rising and setting of certain Stars, and with their position relatively to the Sun, the centre to which they referred the whole starry host, the mind naturally connected the celestial and terrestrial objects that were in fact connected: and they commenced by giving to particular Stars or groups of Stars the names of those terrestrial objects which seemed connected with them; and for those which still remained unnamed by this nomenclature, they, to complete a system, assumed arbitrary and fanciful names.

Thus the Ethiopian of Thebes or Saba styled those Stars under which the Nile commenced to overflow, Stars of Inundation, or that poured out water (AQUARIUS).

Those Stars among which the Sun was, when he had reached the Northern Tropic and began to retreat Southward, were termed, from his retrograde motion, the Crab (CANCER).

As he approached, in Autumn, the middle point between the Northern and Southern extremes of his journeying, the days and nights became equal; and the Stars among which he was then found were called Stars of the Balance (LIBRA).

Those stars among which the Sun was, when the Lion, driven from the Desert by thirst, came to slake it at the Nile, were called Stars of the Lion (LEO).

Those among which the Sun was at harvest, were called those of the Gleaning Virgin, holding a Sheaf of Wheat (VIRGO).

Those among which he was found in February, when the Ewes brought forth their young, were called Stars of the Lamb (Arms).

Those in March, when it was time to plough, were called Stars of the Ox (TAURUS).

Those under which hot and burning winds came from the desert, venomous like poisonous reptiles, were called Stars of the Scorpion (SCORPIO).

Observing that the annual return of the rising of the Nile was always accompanied by the appearance of a beautiful Star, which at that period showed itself in the direction of the sources of that river, and seemed to warn the husbandman to be careful not to be surprised by the inundation, the Ethiopian compared this act of that Star to that of the Animal which by barking gives warning of danger, and styled it the Dog (SIRIUS).[24]

Some symbols were designed to represent the joining of separate aspects. In almost all cases the symbols are older symbols representing a lesson of nature which are joined together to represent relationships or more complex ideas. Here are three examples of this.

The Star of David is a combination of the female and the male aspects joined together to represent the earthly and Divine in harmony. The cross is a combination of the vertical rod representing the Divine and the horizontal bar representing the earthly. The compass creates circles which denote the Divine and the square measures earthly things like wood or stone. The placement of pairs or multiples of symbols in relationship to each other has specific meaning to the communities who created them. In this case all three symbols represent similar aspects but they would not be described as representing the same ideals.

By understanding the original or representative application of a symbol you can discern three things: First, the original, survival based application and real world *lesson of nature* which was being conveyed by the people who designed the symbols to preserve their understanding of nature. Second, by understanding the base application we see the relationship to what the symbol eventually represents after several millennia (i.e. the river stick to the symbol of life or something pointing up representing Deity). Third, we can escape the muddled superstition which accompanies those millennia and see the true *lesson of nature* "hidden" in the symbol or understand the complex relationship of two joined symbols.

Keep these things in mind when conducting the study of symbols and remember that meaning can change, or be changed, over time. Look for the physical representation, practical knowledge, or observation of motion to find the true origins of symbols in order to discover their true and natural secrets. A full study of the symbols found in the 27th degree is recommended.

CHAPTER TEN: NOTES ON NUMBERS AND GEOMETRIC SHAPES

Anyone who has read the 27th degree has encountered the issue of complex and symbolic mathematics in the Scottish Rite. The idea of mathematical symbols providing knowledge and power to those who understand them is as old as watching the moon. Although some of the formulas for the use of mathematics can be complex, understanding the purpose and value of mathematics is not. As with any other symbols the key to understanding is to take the subject to the most practical levels of use. To find the beauty and meaning in the most useful of tools, look for its basic function.

In the ancient world mathematics had only two uses: proportional measurement and predictive analysis. These two aspects allowed scholars to effectively measure movement and time, make art proportional and pleasing to the eye, make tools and machines that fit together, and determine future events based on observations of measureable events in the past.

This was vital to understanding the cycles of the seasons to determine planting times, harvest times, flood times, dry seasons, rainy seasons, and any other of a host of natural phenomenon, the foreknowledge of which, was very helpful to human survival. It was also vital in the construction of straight foundations, sturdy walls, and other necessities of effective construction. The ability of mathematics to assist in meeting the requirements of food, shelter, warmth, and safety soon expanded to other areas of study but its basic function never changed. Even Einstein's study of relativity was based on the mathematical predictive analysis of how light moves in respect to gravity.

Proportional measurement is the ability to form shapes and angles for the purpose of alignment and division. An example of proportional alignment is the ability to form a perfect 90 degree angle in order to make a square corner on a building. An example of proportional division is the ability to form shapes and angles for the purpose of measuring parts of a larger angle. This was required when making 15 degree angles to measure an hour on a sun dial.

Predictive analysis is the ability to determine a future movement or placement based on observations of past movements or placements. In ancient time, in what is now the Middle East, the star Sirius, The Dog Star, appeared in the sky just before the floods came each year. It was seen as a warning of the floods just as a dog barks to warn of danger.[25] In time the learned men of the age discovered how to measure time, to predict when the star would rise and were better able to give warning of the impending floods. The same was true when measuring the movement of the stars and planets, which was used to gauge the time of year for any type of repeating natural events.

The combination of proportional measurement and predictive analysis was used to do everything from telling time, navigating and mapping the earth, and finding one's way home again. As knowledge passed from generation to generation certain numbers and shapes became associated with the lesson of nature they illustrated as well as with aspects of divinity. This lead to mathematics being used in two ways: first, as described above in practical mathematics, and secondly as representative symbols. This second aspect is how we find mathematics sometimes used in Masonry. It is important to understand that Masonry borrowed numbers and shapes from the Sacred Geometry traditions of the past and these ideas are not exclusive to Masonry although sacred geometry was used extensively by Masons.

About numbers

Numbers and counting were the first aspects of deductive thought. All other aspects of ancient life from hunting for food to making art were within the realm of instinct and emotion but the use of numbers and counting represented a quantum leap. Very early in the process numbers took on mystical significance due to the power of advancements that number thought allowed. The ancients believed that something that powerful must be magic. The idea of zero did not develop for a long time but the numerals one through ten held importance from the start. Although numerical meanings differ from culture to culture there were some common similarities.

Odd numbers seem to have been considered more "holy" than even numbers because the first numeral, or "one", most commonly stood for Deity. The numeral three was representative of the power of Deity or the three aspects of Deity. Four was expressive of the four elements of the Earth; earth, fire, water, and air. Five symbolized Earth elements; earth, fire, water, air, and metal, as well as the individual man. In both cases the number five dealt with singular aspects; chemical reactions and the strength or actions of a single man. In this sense five was seen as the microcosm. The numeral six was representative of the male and female forces of nature and the combination of the two. Seen as all things in relation to each other, six was seen in the sense of the macrocosm. Seven signified heaven and earth being the combination of three and four. The numeral seven also came to symbolize higher learning in the seven liberal arts and in the mysteries of nature as displayed in the seven primary colors of the rainbow. Nine was seen as knowledge in general in the sense of worldly skills like agriculture, art, war, cooking, and any other skills found in living. Nine was also important because it was 3X3, both holy and divisible. Ten was all of these things combined back into a Deity number. Remember this when looking at numbers and shapes related to a number. It will assist you in finding the meaning of their use.

The power of knowledge vs. magical numbers

Numerology is the study of the meaning and effects of numbers as predictive tools. Not in the mathematical sense but in a mystical sense. This is especially true in the study of the Kabbalah where the 22 letters of the Hebrew alphabet and their corresponding numbers are combined with the 10 Sephirot, or points, on the Kabbalistic tree to form 32 "paths".

This is important because in this case the numbers are thought to be "magical" or to hold their own power. This is different from mathematics where numbers allow you to work effectively within the rules of the universe. Keep this in mind when reading about numbers because some traditions will attribute the power of nature to the number itself. Remember that there is no such thing as a magical number. This is also true of shapes. Just as with symbols it is the power of the knowledge they represent and not the number or symbol which holds the power. Do not confuse the two.

A student of Masonry will find the symbolism of geometric shapes to be very similar to the representative attributes of the numbers. Be careful in this because some of the number meanings have more depth than the representative shapes. This is especially true of numerology.

About Shapes

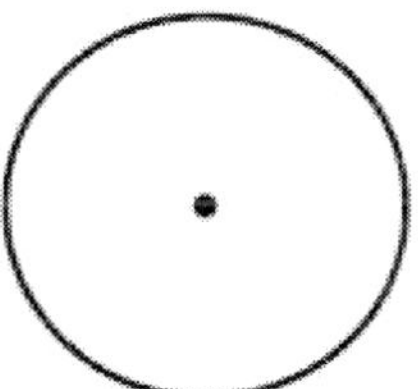

The circumpunct: A point within a circle. In practical terms the idea of the circumpunct is very important. If you try to make a circle by drawing its circumference with a free hand two things will happen. First you will not make a perfect circle, and second you will not be able to create a second circle of the exact same size. Both of these things are required for geometry to work effectively. By using compasses, or a string and stick, a perfect and repeatable circle may be created. In time the point came to represent Deity and the circle came to represent the scope of Divine influence, or all things created. Interestingly in modern astronomy this symbol represents the sun.

The degrees of a circle represent the days in a year when the sun moves. The sun seemed to hold its place in the sky for three days during the summer and winter solstice. The 366 days of the year, minus the 6 the sun did not seem to move, made a circle of 360 points. The 24 hours each represent 15 Degrees of movement. 24 X 15 = 360.

The area of a circle, and the ability to calculate that area was also important. The number 3.141, or Pi, came into importance as a constant for the measurement of the area of a circle.

The Vesica Pisces: This is the "fish" shape created by interlocking two same sized circles with the edges of the circles passing through the center points of the other, or at the center point of the radius. Once this could be accomplished with regularity by an adept they were able to create any angle, shape, or proportion and measure it accurately. For this reason the Vesica Pisces was considered sacred. This was so important that it was considered sacred by many civilizations including Indian, Egyptian, Persian, Tibetan, Chinese, the early Christians, both Gnostic, Urban Roman, and pretty much every other culture which studied mathematics. With it one can make a 90 angle, triangle, square, and create any angle from 0 to 180 with absolute accuracy.

This shape has been incorporated into religious architecture. Almost any church from the middle ages forward includes some form of Vesica Pisces. In many cases it can be found in arches, windows, doors, and other decretive aspects of the building.

  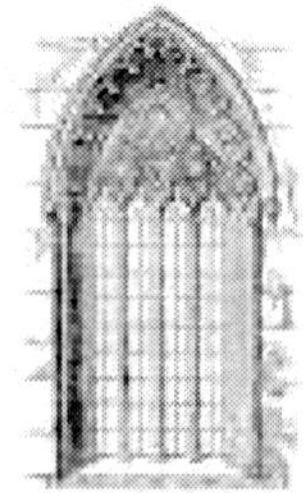

Very soon after men mastered the creation of shapes and their geometrical, or practical, use they started to attribute these created shapes with greater meaning. In many cases shapes were used as secret identifiers between initiates of individual Mystery Schools. A discreetly displayed shape represented some important lesson or principle of training from the school that only another initiate would recognize. The shapes could also demonstrate someone's proficiency in the study of science. This was probably the case with Pythagoras as he traveled the world in search of knowledge. We can surmise that in each case he used these symbols to show his knowledge and worthiness to study with his next new found school. The number of sides the shape had was associated with the meaning attributed to that number. Three is Deity; therefore the triangle represents deity, and so on with each shape.

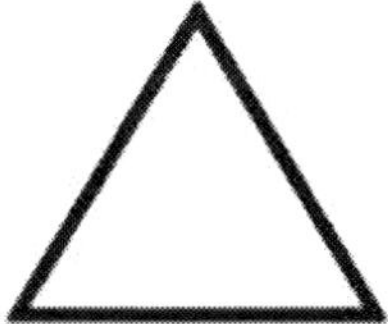

The Equilateral Triangle had the practical use of confirming the accuracy of a circle, the three points touching the circle if it was accurately scribed. It also came to represent the three aspects of Deity: wisdom to create, power to create, and reflection of the creator.

The trinity is seen in many religions as in the Christian ideal of Father, Son, and Holy Ghost as well as the Celtic realms of sky, land, and water.

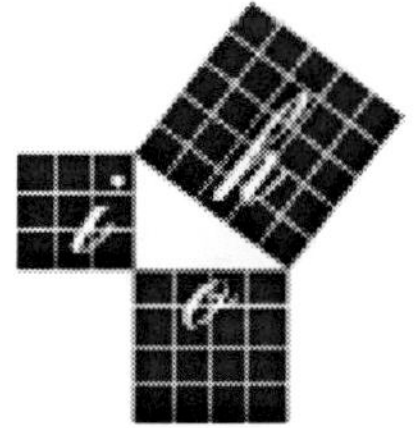

Another very important application of the triangle was the ability to make a 90 degree angle. Once again the aspect of building a straight structure came into play. Pythagoras found that when a triangle had one side of three lengths and another side of four lengths, and was connected with a side of five lengths, a perfect 90 degree angle was created. The three being God, the four being nature, and the five being man made him believe this was a sacred equation.

The Square was important because it was so practical. The sides each had 90 degree angles and it was seen as a place of containment. Just as nature surrounds man, the square came to represent the four elements of the natural world, the FIAT: air - flatus, fire - ignis, water - aqua, and earth - terra. The extension of the square into life was found in man's observations and the lessons of nature.

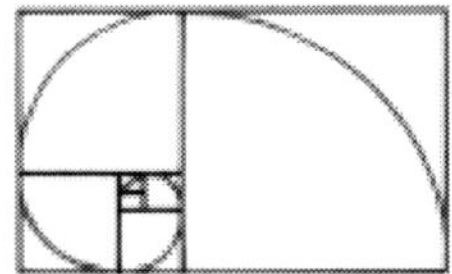

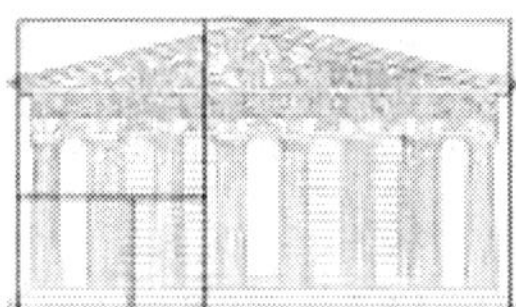

Observations of nature revealed a common ratio in relation to the distribution of life and proportion of nature. This ratio was found in everything from the size of shell growth in the Nautilus fish to the distribution of trees in a forest and even the size of veins and arteries in the human body. The ratio of 1:1.6 is found repeatedly in nature and was considered sacred in ancient times. The creation and use of this ratio became so important that it eventually became known as the Golden Ratio because it provided scale and proportion in synchronization with nature.

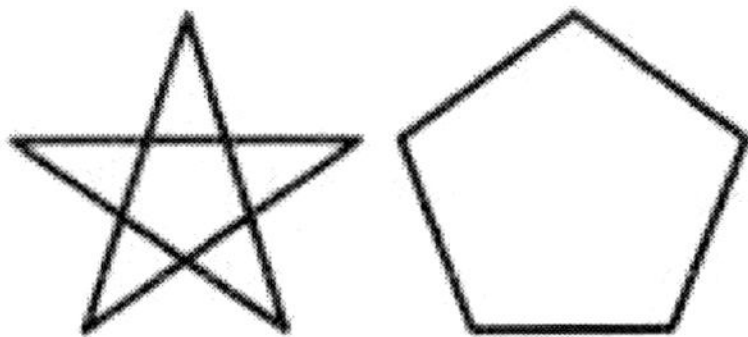

The pentagon and the pentagram were seen as representing man or the efforts of man. It symbolized the five senses as well as the arms, legs, and head of a man. Alchemists attributed four points to the FIAT and the fifth point to the Aether, or spirit aspects of nature. In the case of Masonry it is seen as the aspects of man which must be mastered before a man can move on to understand Deity. The pentagram represents the individual, the microcosm. It is important to remember that this aspect of the individual man means the man within nature, not separate from it. As with all symbols, misinterpretation can lead to misunderstanding the truth.

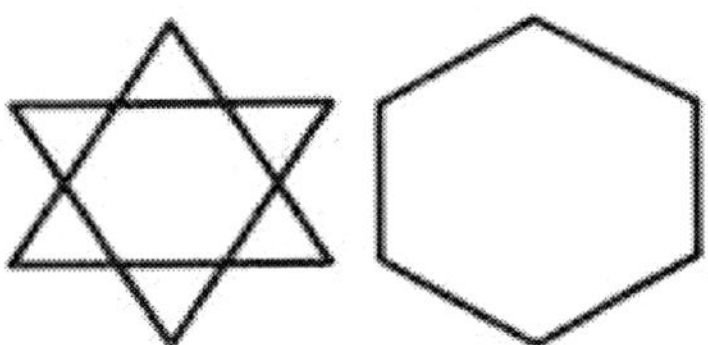

The hexagram and hexagon represents the combining of the male and female aspects in the same way as the number six. Specifically, the male symbol of the triangle point up and the female symbol of triangle point down. This all encompassing aspect signifies the interrelationship of all things in the Macrocosm.

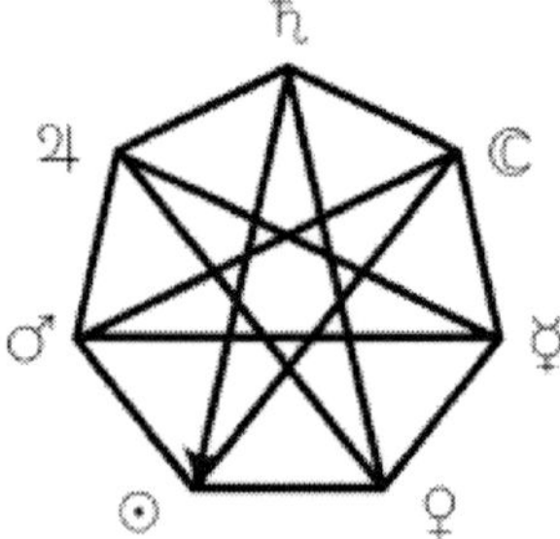

The hectogram and heptagon symbolized the heavens and the earth, being a combination of the three divine aspects and the four earthly elements. It also came to represent higher learning and the seven liberal arts.

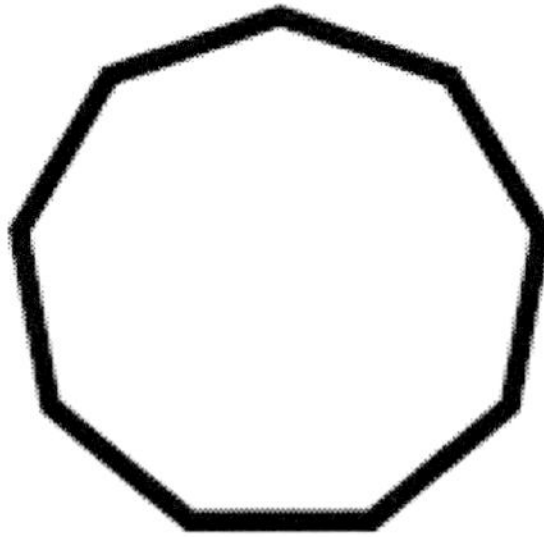

The nonagon is representative of the scope of the world, 3X3, all knowledge within the realm of the living. It was the place of the living and the place we all start from. It was complex to draw and included all other shapes within its generation.

Shapes that represent movement

Some shapes are representative of the path an item takes and the design it makes when the movement is complete. An excellent example of movement representation is the tracing of the movement of the planets. The interior planets, between the earth and the sun, make a rose pattern when looked at in relation to the sun. These "rose" patterns are found with Mercury and Venus. When looked at from the perspective of the earth Venus makes an almost perfect pentagram, moving counter clockwise in its alignment by only two degrees each eight years.

 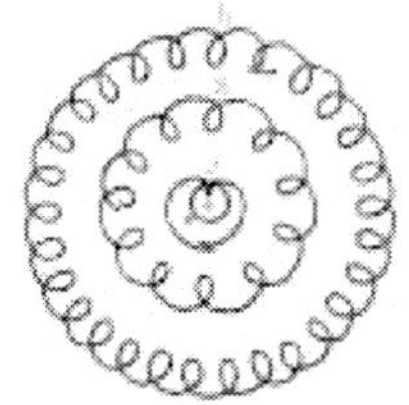

The exterior planets form a tightening circle which represents the visible planets of Mars, Jupiter and Saturn on their path past and beyond the earth. Look for these patterns in the windows of churches and cathedrals. There you will find evidence of a great body of knowledge which was held by the church and other scholars. These patterns are the direct result of mathematical formulas for the prediction of movement of celestial bodies in relation to the earth and sun. This endeavor resulted in the expression of mathematics in its most exquisite representation, as science revealing the beauty and hidden wonder of nature, irrefutable evidence of the wonder of creation.

Conclusion

Mathematics is a tool used by man to understand, predict, and manipulate his world. The importance of mathematics cannot be overstated and it is no wonder man has placed such emphasis, concentration, and value on the meaning of these expressions of the rules of the natural world. This is the key to understanding numbers and geometric shapes. The powers attributed to numbers and geometric shapes are no more than articulations of the functions of numbers combined with the lessons of nature and experiences of man. This representative explanation is man's attempt to find evidence of Deity. Care must be taken in this respect because science cannot prove the existence of God but it can point the way to man's comprehension of, and faith in, Deity as well as man's discovery of the spark of Divinity within himself.

CHAPTER ELEVEN: THE SYMBOLISM OF COLUMNS

The imagery of columns or pillars is used very often in Masonic teaching. It is helpful to understand what message is being expressed or represented by the pillars. Important clues can be found by looking at the type and number of pillars used in the lesson. The terms "column" and "pillar" are used interchangeability in many cases.

The columns introduced in the degrees correspond to style, complexity, and representation of the degrees within Blue Lodge and Scottish Rite Masonry. They are used to represent a variety of ideas spanning the whole range of Masonic study from historical allegory to the Greater Mysteries but in each case their use is uniform in one aspect, columns lift things up.

One broken column represents a lost opportunity to gain more understanding. In Masonry the image of the broken column is most often associated with the death of Grand Master Hiram Abiff but it can also represent any general loss of knowledge or understanding. Note that in the 15th degree we find the columns of the Temple of Perfection thrown down representing change and loss and calling us to rebuild and relearn.

It is thought that the idea of two pillars is as old, or older, than the two pillars representing Upper and Lower Egypt from some 5000 years ago. This tradition of one pillar representing the Strength of Deity and the other representing the Establishment of government were continued through to the time of Solomon and are found in the description of the pillars Jachin and Boaz which stood in front of the Temple of Solomon. In some descriptions, Strength and Establishment held up the mantel over the door which was a symbol of stability for the people of Israel, raising them up among the people of the earth.

Solomon, King Hiram of Tyre, Hiram Abiff are the symbolic link between the two pillars of Strength of Deity and the Establishment of governments or nations and the three pillars of the Kabbalah. In this case King Solomon, the religious leader, is strength, and King Hiram of Tyre, the ruler of men, is establishment. This allowed the enlightened man, Hiram Abiff to flourish. The two pillars provide the stability for the aspects found in the third to flourish.

Pillars found in groups of three are reflections of the three pillars found in the Kabbalistic Tree. The symbolism of the pillars most often signifies some type of balance required to find equilibrium. In the example of Faith, Hope, and Charity we find the virtues of man. With the pillars of Wisdom, Strength, and Beauty we find the attributes of Deity.

To help us find this balance the three pillars serve as a point of reference to the Nine Great Tenets of Masonry described within the degrees. Examples of equilibrium found in the degrees are the requirements between justice and mercy, leadership of others efforts and individual creativeness, and balancing how much you really need versus how much you can give without doing yourself harm. These lessons all eventually lead to ideas addressed in the Greater Mysteries which include our relationship with our fellow man and our relationship with Deity.

The Five Pillars representing the Orders of Architecture are used to describe and categorize the progression of the Seven Liberal Arts that make up the lessons of the Lesser Mysteries. They are also used as waypoints for marking a Mason's progression from the simple strengths of the Lesser Mysteries to the more complex lessons of the Greater Mysteries.

Symbolically, the columns of the five Orders of Architecture are also used to identify the intended purpose of a building. Banks and colleges often have the scholastic representation of scrolled Iconic columns where museums will often have the artistic representation of flowered Corinthian columns. The Supreme Court building in Washington, DC is ornamented with Composite columns to denote the need for the combination of the rule of law and the art of mercy in pursuit of justice.

When reading about columns or pillars take a moment to put the representation of the column in perspective to the intended lesson. Is the lesson a two column lesson about Deity and man speaking to the establishment of governance among men; is it a three column lesson in the esoteric or Kabbalistic tradition; or is it a five column lesson in the Liberal Arts or the Lesser Mysteries? This will help you frame the intent of the lesson.

Descriptions of Jachin and Boaz and the five orders of architecture can be found in the second Fellow Craft Lecture also known as "The Stair Lecture". They are referenced again in the several of the Scottish Rite degrees. Three columns references are found throughout the Blue degree lectures as well as the Scottish Rite degrees.

What follows are brief descriptions of the columns associated with the schools of architecture. These are not complete but will serve you well as a starting place to help you recognize the different types of pillars.[26]

The Tuscan order is very stout, strong and utilitarian, with a plain shaft, a simple capital and base, and is unadorned in all aspects and generally free of any decoration. The Tuscan order is also known as Roman Doric and is actually not as old as the Doric order, but because it is plainer and of a simpler design it is placed first in the order of the columns. The base and capital are both made of series of cylindrical disks of alternating diameter. The shaft is almost never fluted. The proportions vary, but are generally similar to Doric columns. Height to width ratio is about 7:1. It is considered of the male order because it was stronger than the taller, slimmer columns of the later orders. Due to its simplicity and strength it is associated with the first three degrees of Blue Lodge Masonry.

The Doric order is the oldest and simplest of the classical orders. It is composed of a vertical fluted (it has grooves carved up its length) cylinder that is wider at the bottom. It had no detail on its base or capital. It was often topped with an inverted frustum, a shallow cone. It is considered to be of the masculine order because it is often found in the bottom level of ancient buildings, and was therefore considered to be able to hold more weight. The height-to-thickness ratio is about 8:1. The shaft of a Doric column is always fluted. This additional decoration gave way to its status above the Tuscan order. Due to its strength, refinement of fluting, and strong capitals it is associated with the refinement of self found in the degrees of the Lodge of Perfection.

The Ionic column is considerably more complex than the Doric or Tuscan. It usually has a base and the shaft is often fluted. On the top is a capital in the characteristic shape of a scroll, called a volute, at the four corners. The height-to-thickness ratio is around 9:1. Because of the more refined proportions and scroll capitals, the Ionic column is sometimes associated with scholarly or academic endeavors and is often incorporated in the design of buildings used for those purposes. This association with scholarly knowledge lends itself to representing the first two degrees of the Chapter of Rose Croix; the Knight of the East and the Prince of Jerusalem.

The origin of the Corinthian order is not specifically known. It is generally associated with the Greek city-state of Corinth but similar columns were also found in Athens. It is identified as a feminine order because its height to width ratio is about 10:1 making it less sturdy than the Tuscan or Doric orders. The capital was decorated with the leaves of plants and flowers giving it a very complex and artistic design. Due to its association with artistic endeavors it is used in Scottish Rite Masonry to represent the second two degrees of the Chapter of Rose Croix; the Knight of the East and West, and the Knight of Rose Croix.

The Composite order is a mixed order, combining the volutes, or scrolls, of the Ionic order capital with the artistic leaf designs of the Corinthian order. The upper, or capital, aspects of the Composite order are larger than all the other column orders. The column of the Composite order is ten diameters high and always fluted. It is a very ornamental column and is considered a feminine order because it's height to width ratio. Due to its combination of the scholastic and artistic aspects it is representative of the degrees of both the Council of Kadosh and the Consistory which represent training for Knighthood and instruction in the judging of the actions of men.

It is important to remember that these orders have separate distinctions between the purely architectural view and the more symbolic Masonic application. When reading about pillars and architectural orders you may find differences in descriptions, dates of recognition, and time lines of use. Do not let this confuse how they are used in Masonic education. As with many Masonic symbols it is less about historic accuracy and more about its allegorical meaning in Masonry.

CHAPTER TWELVE: CANDIDATE CHARACTERS

The role, or character, the candidate plays within the ceremonies is very important to understanding the situation the candidate is to experience. In the cases where a personal declaration is required the candidate represents himself. At other times the candidate represents a person or situation from history and experiences some tribulation in order to facilitate the learning process of the lesson within the degree.

This is part of the teaching process where the candidate experiences a formative experience from the life or story of the degree character. Albert Pike was convinced that this method of "being in the moment" was the best way to impart the lessons of the degrees.

The descriptions provided here are very cursory and only meant to assist a student in identifying the surroundings and personas involved to "set the stage" of the degree lesson. Careful reading and study are required to glean the fullness of the lessons contained within the degrees. In the ceremonies the candidate finds himself at "a point in time" and learns a lesson or takes an oath that takes him from an incomplete or troubled situation to a complete or resolved situation.

In the ceremonies the person receiving the degree is address by different titles depending upon the goal of the character. He may be called Candidate or Aspirant. Be aware of these titles as they are important to understanding the desired goal of the degree. Candidates are received into the respective bodies for instruction and Aspirants are accepted members expressing a desire for more knowledge or greater responsibility. Take note of the title given in the degree.

The Blue Lodge

1st Degree, Entered Apprentice. The Candidate is in the lodge representing himself.

2nd Degree, Fellow Craft. The Candidate is in the lodge representing himself.

3rd Degree, Master Mason. The setting is the unfinished Temple of Solomon. The candidate represents Hiram Abiff. He starts out alive but is slain by three men representing tyranny, fanaticism, and ignorance. He is not "resurrected" as Hiram Abiff but is "risen" as himself to the sublime degree of a Master Mason, having learned from the experience of the Master's death.

The Lodge of Perfection

4th Degree, Secret Master. The setting is in Solomon's Temple. The candidate is himself. The princes of Israel gather before the drapes of the Holy of the Holies at the loss of Hiram.

They realize the true word is lost. The candidate begins uncommitted to the cause of Masonry, is called to Duty, and ends having committed himself to the requirements of Masonry.

5th Degree, Perfect Master. The setting is in Solomon's Temple and is a reenactment of Hiram's burial on the one year anniversary of his death. The candidate is himself. He begins in a state of procrastination, is called to immediate action, and ends resolved to begin his efforts before the sands of time overtake him.

6th Degree, Intimate Secretary. The setting is in Solomon's Palace. The candidate represents Zabud, a favorite of Solomon. Zabud hears a disturbance in the throne room and in his Zeal to protect King Solomon he is discovered and accused of being a spy. His actions are examined and he is found to be noble and just. He takes the place of the fallen Hiram Abiff as King Solomon's Intimate Secretary.

7th Degree, Provost and Judge. The setting is in Solomon's Temple. The candidate again represents Zabud, this time as an arbitrator of disputes within the Temple. He is asked to show favor to a friend but holds to his honor and judges fairly and impartially. In the end he finds the Recognition of Justice in his role as Provost and Judge.

8th Degree, Intendant of the Building. The setting is in Solomon's Palace. The candidate represents Yehu-aber, a favorite of Hiram Abiff. The work on the Temple must continue and King Solomon seeks new leadership to oversee the work. Five young men are identified as having been the favorites of the Grand Master for their skill and desire to learn. The candidate learns the meaning of Stewardship and becomes one of five Intendants of the Building.

9th Degree, Elu of the Nine. The setting is in Solomon's palace and in a cave in the wilderness. The candidate again represents Yehu-aber who had been selected to be an Intendant of the Building. A herdsman finds the assassins and reports them to King Solomon. Nine are sent to find them. One assassin is found and slain. The candidate is selected as one of the Elu of the Nine and learns skills in how to Judge.

10th Degree, Elu of the Fifteen. The setting is in the Wilderness and then in Solomon's Palace. The candidate again represents Yehu-aber, one of the Elu of the Nine. The two remaining assassins are discovered in the land of Gath. The Elu of the nine and 6 others are dispatched to recover them. The ruffians are captured, tried, and executed. The candidate is made one of the Elu of the Fifteen and learns lessons about where to Judge.

11th Degree, Elu of the Twelve. The setting is in Solomon's Audience Chamber.The candidate represents Ben-Dekar, One of the Elu of the Nine, Twelve, and Fifteen. Justice being done to the assassins, King Solomon learns of unjust tax collectors in his kingdom. He sends 12 of the 15 Elu to be his AMETH in Israel. The candidate learns when to Judge and ends the degree by becoming a Governor in Israel and chief over the collection of revenue.

12th Degree, Master Architect. The setting is in Solomon's Temple. The candidate represents Adoniram, one of five Intendants of the Building. Adoniram is recognized as being a wise leader and he is raised above his peers due to his skill and knowledge. In the end the candidate is the new Master Architect of the Temple replacing the murdered Hiram Abiff.

13th Degree, The Royal Arch of Solomon. The setting is the ruins of Enoch's temple. There is a requirement for three candidates to represent Adoniram, Yehu-Aber, and Satolkin. The three candidates search for the Lost Word in the deep vertical vault under Enoch's crypt. On the third try, with the aid of light, they find the Lost Word and take it to King Solomon. The candidate begins by searching and discovers honor and fidelity in learning. In the end he has found something but knows he does not possess an understanding of what he has found.

14th Degree, Perfect Elu. The setting is Solomon's sacred vault. The candidate is himself. The candidate discovers the Lost Word of God in a Horizontal vault under Solomon's temple. The candidate learns that finding is not always the same as understanding. Completion of one's personal Temple is the key to understanding.

The Chapter of Rose Croix

15th Degree, Knight of the East. The setting is the Ruined Temple of Solomon and later, the Court of King Cyrus. The candidate represents Zerubbabel, a man of the House of Solomon, and a Prince in Israel. Zurubbabel returns to Jerusalem to rebuild the Temple. He risks his own freedom for the freedom of others. By placing service before self he gains permission to rebuild the Temple and secures freedom for his people.

16th Degree, Prince of Jerusalem. The setting is the Ruined Temple, the Hall of the West and Cyrus's Court in the East. The candidate represents Kadmiel ben Zabud. He travels to Jerusalem and offers to assist in the rebuilding of the Temple. He finds the Jews are hindered in their rebuilding of the Temple by Sumerians. Kadmiel ben Zabud is there to witness how Zurubbabel wins King Darius's favor through his wisdom. In the end the candidate learns about the strength of wisdom and resolution in making goals into realities.

17th Degree, Knight of the East and West. The setting is the Council Chamber of the Knights. The candidate is himself. In the beginning he is undeclared. The candidate is a lost soul wondering alone beside a sea of false philosophies. He is asked questions of his dedication to Masonry. Messages of repentance are recited to the candidate. Through acceptance and humility he ends the ceremony with a new declaration of dedication.

18th Degree, Knight of Rose Croix. The setting progresses through Three Chambers, Tyranny of Evil, Passions, and Freedom from evil. The candidate is himself. In the beginning the candidate is committed to himself and his brothers but through transformation he comes out committed to all mankind.

The Council of Kadosh

19th Degree, Grand Pontiff (Bridge builder). The setting is the Court of the Knights of St. Andrew. The candidate is himself. The Knight of St. Andrew is received and waits in contemplation of New Jerusalem. The 12 pillars are explained to him. He is then plunged into darkness and silence, evil comes upon him, but, by the candidate's valor evil is destroyed. This is the rebuilding the Temple within himself. It begins the candidate's Path Forward as a builder of the New City. In the end he is made a Priest of the Order of Melchizedek.

20th Degree, Master of the Symbolic Lodge. The setting is the Council Chamber of the Knights of Kadosh. The candidate is himself. The candidate is surrounded by nine unlit candles and three pillars. The three pillars are explained as the foundation of the fraternity; the nine candles are lit and explained as the nine great truths of Masonry. The candidate begins committed but untutored. He learns the methods of Noble Interactions and in the end is ennobled with knowledge of truth.

21st Degree, Nocahite or Prussian Knight. The setting is in the Tribunal of the Prussian Knights. The candidate represents Adolf, a Knight of the Crusades. The Knight returns from the crusades to find his lands stolen by false documentation. He is heard in a tribunal and the truth comes out through trial of the false Count. The Knight is asked to replace the false Count on the tribunal. Through his trust in God his lands and holdings are returned and his nobility earns him a place of honor on the Tribunal.

22nd Degree, Knight Royal Axe or Prince of Libanus. The setting is in the Carpenter's workshop and then at the round table in the Council room of the Carpenter's. The candidate represents a Prussian Knight. The candidate demands to be made a Prince of Libanus by birth and rank. He is denied and must set aside birth and rank and labor beside the workmen to gain their respect and unanimous permission to be raised to the position of Prince of Libanus. He is transformed through labor and humility from demanding honors to a place where he is worthy of honors.

23rd Degree, Chief of the Tabernacle. The setting is first in the Court of the Tabernacle and then in the tabernacle of Moses. The candidate represents Eliaseph the Levite. The candidate, a Levite, learns of the death of fellow Levites who rebelled against authority. In darkness the candidate is purified and is warned to approach the Mysteries with sincerity to serve God. He learns of the Lesser Mysteries of the Hebrew and Judaic tradition. Through his dedication to the respectful study of the Mysteries he is accepted as a Chief of the Tabernacle.

24th Degree, Prince of the Tabernacle. The setting is the Court of the Tabernacle and in the vestibule of the Tabernacle. The candidate represents Phinehas, Son of Eleazar of the house of Aaron. The candidate stands before Celeb and promises to make reparation for any wrong he has done. On this promise he is instructed in reason, liberty, and faith. He is then tested by air, water and fire with moral lessons given at each test. He raises Osiris from the dead not with reason or logic but with faith. He begins uninitiated in the mysteries but through philosophical lessons in the Greater mysteries of the great societies he learns to Know, to Will, to Dare, and to Be Silent.

25th Degree, Knight of the Brazen Serpent. The setting is the Houses of the Earth, Planets, and the Sun & Moon, (Light). The candidate represents Idris. He sits in darkness to reflect for five minutes in rooms of the earth, planets, and sun. He writes down his faults and chooses one of them to master. He vows to govern his life by virtue. He declares his faith in Deity in writing and receives a white turban of purity of faith. He begins as unschooled in the stars but through the study of the Greater mysteries of the Islamic faith he is introduced to astronomy. He learns about the strength to be gained from overcoming his own weaknesses.

26th Degree, Prince of Mercy or Scottish Trinitarian. The setting is in the Catacombs under Rome. The candidate represents Constance, a Catechumen who seeks to become one of the faithful. He washes his hands and is told to clean his soul as well. Nine rounds for nine lessons of the Trinity, three affirmations of his search for truth, the final mystery is revealed, Resurrection. Water on his head purifies his soul. A tau cross is placed on his forehead. All partake of bread and wine. In this way the faithful are introduced to the Greater mysteries of Christian faith and instructed in the Trinity.

Note: In 2004 the order of presentation of the 27th and the 28th degrees were reversed. The degrees are unchanged in ceremony, only the order of presentation is changed. This was done for the sake of continuity on the recommendation of Dr. Hutchens and the authority of the Supreme Council, Southern Jurisdiction. This was not change for the sake of change. It was the result of rational thinking. The 23rd through the 26th degrees are philosophical mystery degrees, as is the Knight of the Sun, Prince Adept. It made sense to group them together. By the same logic the 29th and 30th degrees are chivalric, as is the Knight Commander of the Temple. It represents the vigil preformed prior to a knighting ceremony. To align the degrees with the adjacent lessons the order was reversed. The Knight of the Sun, Prince Adept became the 27th degree and the Knight Commander of the Temple became the 28th degree. There is a lot of material from before 2004 which shows the degrees in the old sequence. Understand the change and why it was done.

27th Degree, Knight of the Sun, Prince Adept. The candidate is himself. The setting is the Lodge of the Council of Kadosh and the Houses of the Planets. The Candidate affirms his willingness to overcome prejudices with reason. He carves favors in stone and injuries in sand. He is told that a man binds himself in life with false restraints. He travels to seven Houses of the Planets for instruction from the Kabbalah. He begins bond by earthly notions but learns vision through the wisdom introduced in the Kabbalah. In the end his mind is freed and his training for knighthood is declared complete.

28th Degree, Knight Commander of the Temple. The setting is the vigil chamber of the Chapter of Commanders. The Candidate, Constans, a Prince of Mercy, seeks to become Knight Commander of the Temple. He drinks wine, and eats bread and salt. He admits his faults and promises to amend them. He then holds vigil. Many temptations call to him but he leaves his vigil only to save the city from attack. He is found worthy and advanced to the rank he seeks. He begins untested in his resolve to become a knight, but through the call to leadership he is found worthy, wise, and faithful. He is made a Knight Commander of the Temple.

29th Degree, Scottish Knight of St. Andrew. The setting is the Court of the Knights of St. Andrew. The candidate is himself. The candidate enters a room with a candle at the corners of the alter representing chivalric duties. In a second room the candidate is put to inquisition. He then washes and learns more qualities of knighthood. He begins as untested in his resolve to keep his faith but through his dedication he shows the qualities of knighthood and is made a Knight of St. Andrew.

30th Degree, Knight Kadosh, The setting is in a tomb and then in the Court of the Knights of Kadosh. The candidate is himself. The candidate is girded for combat but finds the battle is with himself. He encounters the spirit of a fallen candidate who warns him to not proceed, for if he is not pure of heart and wholly committed he will die. When he overcomes his fear of death he is warned to set his house in order and that a knight's work is never done. He departs the spirit and encounters the frank judges. He is challenged and declared dependable. He receives more instruction on the seven liberal arts. He begins untested, is challenged by death and, if successful, ends by being made a Knight Kadosh.

The Consistory

31st Degree, Inspector Inquisitor. The setting is an Egyptian tomb which transforms into the Hall of Justice where the Egyptian Court of the Dead is held. The candidate represents Cheres, Son of Suphis, who is recently deceased. The candidate is a soul at its last judgment. He is called to answer for all he has done in life. He begins with his soul untested, learns what it is like to be judged fairly and, in the end, receives his final judgment.

32nd Degree, Master of the Royal Secret. The setting is in a Court of the Consistory set before the Camp of Scottish Rite Masonry. The candidate is himself. The candidate is taught the nature of man's relationship with God and then shown the camp. He sees, for the first time, the scope and extent of the many bodies he has encountered in his advancement in Masonry. He learns the value of Equilibrium, Balance, and Harmony. His journey is culminated as he becomes a Master of the Royal Secret.

The Master of the Royal Secret now has a lifetime of study and reflection to enjoy as he seeks to better understand all the things he has learned.

CHAPTER THIRTEEN
THE ELU DEGREES

In the degrees of the Lodge of Perfection we follow the lives of the Fellow Craft of the Temple of Solomon. In the tracking of the members of the respective Elu degrees we follow the progression (or demise) of the Fellow Craft working in the Temple of Solomon. The three ruffians are from this group and fall victim to the vices and folly of men. They conspire to force the Master's word from the Grand Master Hiram Abiff and fail epically as they become frustrated and kill him when he refuses to relent to their threats.

Ruffians

Jubela-Guibs - Conspirator, (Fanaticism)
Jubelo-Gravelot - Conspirator, (Despotism)
Jubelum-Akirop - Slayer of the Grand Master, (Ignorance)

The remaining Fellow Craft are of nobler moral character and represent the positive virtues which Freemasonry promotes. By following their progress and understanding their roles in the degrees we are offered a perspective on the development and advancement of these men and so can better understand the lessons they represent.

Five Favorites

As described in the 8th degree, Hiram Abiff had five young men with whom he worked closely and who were believed to have been involved with the building of the Temple from the start. These men take different roles at different times and represent a variety of positive attributes. Solomon says: "His [Hiram's] chief favorites were Adoniram Ben Abada, Yehu-aber the noble Phoenician, Satolkin of the Tribe of Benjamin, Zelec the Phoenician from Gebal, and Gareb of the Tribe of Napthali, to whom he taught all the learning that he had gathered from the wisdom of Egypt. He often spoke to me of these his scholars, saying that when he was dead, they would be able to take his place".

It is assumed that the five favorites are members of the Elu of the Nine and so are included in the Elu of the Fifteen. As the Elu of the Twelve are identified by name it is believed that the three favorites not named as Elu of the Twelve remain with the Temple of Solomon. Satolkin ben Hesed and Yehu-aber ben Hur eventually move on to Israel as Elu of the Twelve but Adoniram ben Abada, Zelec the Phoenician, and Gareb of the Tribe of Napthali appear to have not left the Temple. Note that Yehuaber is not a manager of other men but an artisan. Here is the lesson that the skilled laborer is honored among men.

1. Adoniram ben Abada - Replaces Hiram Abiff as Master Architect of the Temple.
2. Zelec the Phoenician from Gebal - Chief of the stonemasons.
3. Gareb of the Tribe of Napthali - Chief of the workmen in silver and gold and the engravers.

4. Satolkin ben Hesed - Chief of works in Wood.
5. Yehu-aber ben Hur –Artificer in Brass. He is also the Elu who finds and kills Jubela-Guibs.

Elu of the Nine

9th Degree, Nine wise men who are sent by King Solomon to collect the Ruffians from Gath. They find and kill Jubela-Guibs. They represent the Upper House or Senate which is made up of older learned men who serve longer terms.

1. Adoniram ben Abada*
2. Zelec the Phoenician*
3. Gareb of the Tribe of Napthali*
4 .Yehu-aber ben Hur
5. Ben-Dekar
6. Satolkin ben Hesed
7. Zerbal ben Abinadab
8. Unidentified
9. Unidentified

*Although it is not specifically stated, it is assumed that these favorites were, along with Yehu-aber and Satilkin, involved with the capture of the ruffians and included in the Elu of the Nine and Fifteen. Pharos, the herdsman, is not a member of the Temple and therefore not an Elu. The names of the last two Elu of the Nine, which are not provided in the text of the ceremonies, are among the eight additional names provided as Elu of the Fifteen.

Elu of the Fifteen

10th Degree, Fifteen wise men who are sent to collect the remaining two Ruffians from Gath. The Elu capture Jubelo Gravelot and Jubelum-Akirop, returning them to King Solomon's court for trial. They are found guilty and executed. These fifteen represent the younger men of a Lower House of Representatives or House of the Common Man who serve for shorter terms.

1. Adoniram ben Abada*
2. Zelec the Phoenician*
3. Gareb of the Tribe of Napthali*
4. Satolkin ben Hesed
5. Yehu-aber ben Hur
6. Ben-Dekar
7. Zerbal ben Abinadab
8. Abner ben Geber
9. Ahimaz
10. Ahinadab ben Iddo
11. Bana ben Ahilud
12. Banah ben Hushai
13. Geber ben Uri
14. Shimei ben Elah
15. Yosaphat ben Paruah

Elu of the Twelve

11th & 12th Degree, Selected from the Elu of the Fifteen by King Solomon to serve as Governors of Israel. They represent trial by jury and a separate judicial branch.

1. Abner ben Geber
2. Ahimaz
3. Ahinadab ben Iddo
4. Bana ben Ahilud
5. Banah ben Hushai
6. Ben-Dekar
7. Geber ben Uri
8. Satolkin ben Hesed
9. Shimei ben Elah
10. Yehu-aber ben Hur
11. Yosaphat ben Paruah

12. Zerbal ben Abinadab

Enoch's Temple

13th Degree. Before departing for Israel Yehu-aber and Satolkin join Adoniram for the search of Enoch's temple and discover the lost word.

1. Adoniram ben Abada,
2. Yehu-Aber ben Hur,
3. Satolkin ben Hesed,

These are characters of action and ability who labor honorably for their Deity and their fellow man. Study their lives, both failings and accomplishments, in order that you may emulate their virtues and avoid their mistakes.

APPENDIX:
GLOSSARY OF NAMES

Listed below are the names of significant characters from the degrees. Officers of the respective bodies are not specifically identified in this list. The degrees in which the character plays a part are listed after the name. A brief description of the character or their role in the degree is provided.

Glossary

Aaron - 23, Brother of Moses and Venerable High Priest of the Tabernacle.

Abairam - 23, With Datham he lead a layman's revolt against the civil authority claimed by Moses.

Abdullah - 25, Friend of Idris, introduces him to the Sufi Masters.

Abner ben Geber - 11, One of the Elu of the Fifteen chosen to be one of the Elu of the Twelve.

Adolf - 21, Knight of the Crusades who returns home to find his land and holdings unjustly taken by Reinfred.

Adoniram ben Abada - 5, 8, 11, 12, One of five young men favored by Hiram Abiff for their love of learning. A workman in the Temple, he replaces Hiram Abiff as Master Architect of the Temple.

Ahaiah - 7, Junior Inspector of the Temple.

Ahimaz - 11, One of the Elu of the Fifteen chosen to be one of the Elu of the Twelve.

Ahinadab ben Iddo - 11, One of the Elu of the Fifteen chosen to be one of the Elu of the Twelve.

Alfred - 19, Wise man of England, Just King of Saxon England.

Alihoreph - 7, Senior Inspector of the Temple.

Anubis - 31, Black headed, Jackal faced, God of the Dead, son of Nephthys.

Arial the Elder - 16, Expert of the Council of Knights of the East.

Asher - 19, 22, Tribe of Israel, North-Northwest, Tree.
Atum - 31, God of creation, finisher of the world.
Azariah - 7, Chief Provost of the Temple.
Bana ben Ahilud - 11, One of the Elu of the Fifteen chosen to be one of the Elu of the Twelve.
Banah - 15, Captain of the Guard in the palace if Cyrus, King of Persia.
Banah ben Hushai - 11, One of the Elu of the Fifteen chosen to be one of the Elu of the Twelve.
Banaias - 9, 10, 11, 12, Captain of the Host in the Temple.
Ben-Dekar - 11, One of the Elu of the Nine and Fifteen chosen to be one of the Elu of the Twelve.
Benjamin - 19, 22, Tribe of Israel, Northwest, Wolf.
Bishop of Vienna - 21, The Bishop of Vienna and Count Reinfred of Loëgria who, by unjust means, took the land and holdings of Adolf.
Brother Truth - 27, Introduction for the Choir of Angels.
Caleb - 24, Master of Ceremonies in the Tabernacle. Not of the Tribe of Judah but praised as a servant of God. Represents the acceptance of all good men.
Cassiel - 27, Angel of the Choir.
Cheres - 31, Son of Suphis, deceases and in the Egyptian Court of the Dead.
Confucius - 19, Wise man of China.
Constance - 26, A Catechumen who seeks to become one of the faithful.
Constance - 27, Prince of Mercy.
Cyrus - 15, King of Persia, at the city of Babylon.
Dan - 19, 22, Tribe of Israel, North, Eagle.
Darius - 16, King of Persia, at the city of Babylon (After Cyrus).
Dathan - 23, With Abairam he lead a layman's revolt against the civil authority claimed by Moses.
Duamutef - 31, Son of Osiris, head of a Jackal. Stands in the east.
Eleazar - 23, Son of Aaron and Excellent Priest of the Tabernacle.
Eliaseph the Levite - 23, The candidate for the first degree (lowest) of Judaic Priesthood.

Elu of the Fifteen – 10, Fifteen wise men who represent the Lower House, Serve for shorter terms, they are younger men.
Elu of the Nine - 9, Nine wise men who are sent to collect the Ruffians from Gath. They represent the Upper House, Serve longer terms and are older and wiser than the other Elus.
Elu of the Twelve - 11, 12, Governors of Israel chosen from the Elu of the Fifteen, They represent trial by jury and a separate judicial branch.
Ephraim - 19, 22, Tribe of Israel, West, Bull.
Esdras - 16, A brother of the Temple.
Father Adam - 27, Master of the Choir of Angels.
Gabriel - 27, Angel of the Choir.
Gad - 19, 22, Tribe of Israel, Southwest, Stars.
Gareb of the tribe of Napthali - 8, One of five young men favored by Hiram Abiff for their love of learning, Chief of works in silver and gold & the engravers. One of the Elu of the Nine and Fifteen.
Geber ben Uri - 11, One of the Elu of the Fifteen chosen to be one of the Elu of the Twelve.
Haggai - 16, The Scribe of the Council of Knights of the East.
Hammurabi - 19, Wise man of Babylon, King and lawgiver of the Babylonians.
Hanael - 27, Angel of the Choir.
Hananiah - 16, A brother of the Temple.
Hapy - 31, Son of Osiris, head of an Ape. Stands in the north.
Hermes - 19, Wise man of Egypt and Greece, he whom the Egyptians called Thoth, and the Greeks Hermes.
Herod - 17, King Herod the II of Jerusalem, Slayer of John the Baptist.
Hiram of Tyre - 5, 6, 8-13, King of Tyre and Friend to King Solomon.
Horus - 31, Son of Isis and Osiris, he has the head of a hawk. Presents the deceased to the Court of the Dead.
Idris - 25, Candidate for the mysteries.
Imsety - 31, Son of Osiris, head of a Human. Stands in the south.

Isis - 31, Queen Isis, Goddess of Magic and motherhood, sister and wife of the King Osiris, Mother of Horus.
Issachar - 19, 22, Tribe of Israel, Northeast, Ass.
Ithamar - 23, Son of Aaron and Excellent Priest of the Tabernacle.
Jarib - 16, Jarib the Elder, of the Council of Knights of the East.
Jarib the Elder - 16, Assistant Expert of the Council of Knights of the East.
Joshua - 16, The High-Priest of the Council of Knights of the East.
Jubela-Guibs - 9, 10, Conspirator, (Fanaticism).
Jubelo-Gravelot - 9, 10, Conspirator, (Despotism).
Jubelum-Akirop - 9, 10, Slayer of the Grand Master, (Ignorance).
Judah - 19, 22, Tribe of Israel, East, Lion.
Kadmiel ben Zabud (See Zabud) - 16, Candidate for the mysteries of the Knights of the East.
Kebehsenuef - 31, Son of Osiris, head of a Hawk. Stands in the west.
Korah - 23, Lead a revolt among the Levites contesting the religious authority of Moses and the Aaronites.
Leivites - 23, Holy men who served within the Tabernacle. Served as subordinate officials, under High Priests and Priests, in charge of the lower duties of the sanctuary.
Lieutenant Commander - 21, Prussian Knight.
Maat - 31, Egyptian Goddess of Truth.
Makah - 10, Ruler of Gath.
Manassah - 19, 22, Tribe of Israel, South-Southwest, Vine.
Manu - 19, Wise Indian, most ancient legislator of the Aryans of India.
Marshal - 21, Prussian Knight.
Michal - 27, Angel of the Choir.
Mordecai - 16, A brother of the Temple.
Moses - 14, 19, Law giver of the Hebrews.
Naboth - 7, Master Mason and foreman of labor at the Temple.
Naphtali - 19, 22, Tribe of Israel, North-Northeast, Deer.
Nephthys - 31, Goddess of the Night and Lamentation, sister of

Isis, portrayed as a young. woman, wearing a headdress in the shape of a house and basket.

Numa - 19, Wise man of Rome, Just and wise king of Rome.

Osiris - 31, Head of the Court of the Dead.

Pharos - 9, 10, a herdsman who discovers the cave of the ruffian Jubelum-Akirop.

Phinehas - 24, Son of Eleazar of the house of Aaron.

Prince Esdras - 16, Secretary of the Council of Knights of the East.

Prince Hananiah - 16, Treasurer of the Council of Knights of the East.

Prince Hasim - 16, Almoner of the Council of Knights of the East.

Prince Mordecai - 16, Junior Warden of the Council of Knights of the East.

Prince Nehemiah - 16, Guardian of the Temple of the Council of Knights of the East.

Prince Salamial - 16, Master of Ceremonies of the Council of Knights of the East.

Prince Seraiah - 16, Senior Warden of the Council of Knights of the East.

Rachel - 15, Wife of Zerubbabel.

Raphael - 27, Angel of the Choir.

Reinfred - 21, Count Reinfred of Loëgria and the Bishop of Vienna who by unjust means took the land and holdings of Adolf.

Reuben - 19, 22, Tribe of Israel, South, Man.

Sachiel - 27, Angel of the Choir.

Salamial - 16, A Prince of Israel who introduces Kadmiel ben
Zabud to the Council of the Knights of the East.

Satolkin ben Hesed of the tribe of Benjamin - 8, 9, 10, 11, One of five young men favored by Hiram Abiff for their love of learning, Chief of works in Wood, One of the Elu of the Nine and Fifteen. Chosen to be one of the Elu of the Twelve. Accompanies the Candidate into the cave of the ruffian Jubelum-Akirop.

Shimei ben Elah - One of the Elu of the Fifteen chosen to be one of the Elu of the Twelve.

Simeon - 19, 22, Tribe of Israel, South-Southeast, Sword.
Solomon - 5, 6, 8-13, King of Israel, Builder of the Temple.
St. John the Evangelist - 17, Biblical figure revered in Masonry
Sufi Master, First - 25, Wise man of Islam.
Sufi Master, Fourth - 25, Wise man of Islam.
Sufi Master, Second - 25, Mullah Nasruddin, Wise man of Islam.
Sufi Master, Third - 25, Wise man of Islam.
Thoth - 31, Head of an Ibis, God of wisdom and the moon, Scribe of the Egyptian Gods.
Tsadoc - 8, High Priest of the Temple.
Uriah - 7, Operative Mason with a labor dispute in the Temple.
Warden - 21, Prussian Knight.
Warden of the North - 21, Prussian Knight.
Warden of the South - 21, Prussian Knight.
Yehu-aber ben Hur (the Phoenician) - 8, 9, 10, 11, Elu of the Nine who finds and kills Jubela-Guibs. One of five young men favored by Hiram Abiff for their love of learning, Artificer in Brass. One of the Elu of the Nine, Fifteen, and Twelve.
Yosaphat - 7, 11, 12, Recorder.
Yosaphat ben Paruah – 11, One of the Elu of the Fifteen chosen to be one of the Elu of the Twelve.
Zabud (See Kadmeil ben Zabud) - 5, 6, 7, 11, 12, A favorite of King Solomon who becomes his Intimate Secretary.
Zamael - 27, Angel of the Choir.
Zarathustra - 19, Wise Persian, Bactrian soldier and King.
Zebulon - 19, 22, Tribe of Israel, Southeast, Ship.
Zelec the Pheinician from Gareb – 8, One of five young men favored by Hiram Abiff for their love of learning, Chief of works in Stone. One of the Elu of the Nine, and Fifteen.
Zerbal - 6, Captain of the Guard.
Zerbal ben Abinadab -11, One of the Elu of the Fifteen chosen to be one of the Elu of the Twelve.
Zerubbabel - 15, 16, One of the House of Solomon, and a Prince in Israel, The Governor of the Council of Knights of the East.

BRIDGE BUILDERS GUIDE BIBLIOGRAPHY

Bibliography alphabetically:

Albert Pike. *Morals and Dogma of the Ancient and Accepted Scottish Rite of Freemasonry*. Supreme Council of the Southern Jurisdiction, AASR, USA, 1871.

http://www.alchemywebsite.com/index.html /.

Auturo De Hoyos. *Albert Pike's Esoterika, The Symbolism of the Blue Lodge Degrees*. Scottish Rite Research Society, Washington, DC 2008.

Dennis William Hauck, *The complete Idiot's Guild to Alchemy*, Penguin Group New York, New York, 2008.

Grace F. Knoche, *The Mystery Schools*. by Theosophical University Press. 1999.

Julian Small, *The Five Orders of Classical Architecture*, http://www.cadking.co.uk. 2011.

Nicholas Barnaud Delphinas, *The Book of Lambspring*, 1607.

Pir-o-Murshid Inayat Khan, *A Sufi Message of Spiritual Liberty*, London 1914.

Supreme Council of the Southern Jurisdiction, AASR, Degrees of the Scottish Rite, 2004.

Timothy Hogan, T*he 32 secret paths of Solomon, A new examination of the Qabballah in Freemasonry*, 2009.

Timothy Hogan, *The alchemical keys to Masonic ritual*, 2007.

Waszu-Barrett, Wendy Rae, *Theatrical Interpretations of the Indispensable Degrees, Heredom*, 2004, Vol 12.

NOTES

1. Albert Pike. *Morals and Dogma of the Ancient and Accepted Scottish Rite of Freemasonry*. Supreme Council of the Southern Jurisdiction, AASR, USA, 1871, p iv.
2. Ibid. p 148.
3. Supreme Council of the Southern Jurisdiction, AASR, Degrees of the Scottish Rite, 2004, 32nd Degree.
4. Pike. *Morals and Dogma*. p 356.
5. Waszu-Barrett, Wendy Rae, "Theatrical Interpretations of the Indispensable Degrees", *Heredom*, 2004, Vol 12, p 145.
6. Ibid. p 145.
7. Pike. *Morals and Dogma*. p. 356.
8. Waszu-Barrett, "Theatrical Interpretations". p 148.
9. Ibid. p 145.
10. I will not specifically reference these texts as they are the old ceremonies which have, for the most part, been collected into the House of the Temple. Suffice to say they are not the concise degrees we enjoy today.
11. The references here are too vast to document and sighting one sources on the Masonic aspect of the Hero's Quest is very unfair to all the other writers. Seek these writers out and learn what they have to offer.
12. Timothy Hogan, *The 32 secret paths of Solomon, A new examination of the Qabballah in Freemasonry*, 2009. p 13.
13. Timothy Hogan, *The alchemical keys to Masonic ritual*, 2007. Pp 9-10.
14. From http://www.alchemywebsite.com/index.html /.
15. Nicholas Barnaud Delphinas, *The Book of Lambspring*, 1607.
16. Supreme Council of the Southern Jurisdiction, AASR, Degrees of the Scottish Rite, 2004, 24th Degree.
17. Auturo De Hoyos. *Albert Pike's Esoterika, The Symbolism of the Blue Lodge Degrees*. Scottish Rite Research Society, Washington, DC 2008, Pp 120-122.
18. Ibid. Pp 116-120.
19. Ibid. Pp 119-121.
20. Ibid. Pp 121-123.
21. Dennis William Hauck, *The complete Idiot's Guild to Alchemy*, Penguin Group New York, New York, 2008. p 61.

22. Pir-o-Murshid Inayat Khan, *A Sufi Message of Spiritual Liberty*, London 1914.
23. Grace F. Knoche, *The Mystery Schools*. by Theosophical University Press. 1999, Chapter 7.
24. Pike. *Morals and Dogma*. Pp. 445-446.
25. Ibid. p 446.
26. Julian Small, *The Five Orders of Classical Architecture*, http://www.cadking.co.uk. 2011.

ABOUT THE AUTHOR

Brother Kyle G. Ferlemann is a perpetual life member of Golden Rule Lodge #90 in Topeka, Kansas and a Knight of St. Andrew in Scottish Rite Valley of Topeka in the Orient of Kansas. His formal education includes advanced military studies and degrees in psychology and criminal justice. A lifelong martial scientist his eclectic studies range from military history and counter insurgency to Taoist philosophy and moving meditation. He serves his Lodge and Valley as a Masonic education lecturer and contributing writer for various masonic periodicals. A Pipefitter by trade and a Soldier by profession he has deployed extensively into post conflict areas of Europe and Asia to assist in rebuilding nations and social stability. He is an accomplished Soldier, teacher, and author as well as an avid student of life and light.

His curiosity about the teachings of Masonry prompted him to explore the rational and methods of Masonic education. As a military trainer and college instructor his strength is the ability to articulate complex ideas and motivations in understandable, real world terms. These aspects joined in the creation of his third book, and first full length Masonic work, The Bridge Builder's Guide; A study companion for the degrees of the Southern Jurisdiction of Scottish Rite Masonry.

More Books in the Cornerstone
Scottish Rite Education Series

The Lodge of Perfection
by Albert Pike
Foreword by Michael R. Poll
6x9 Softcover 152 pages
ISBN 1-934935-13-1

Book of the Ancient and Accepted Scottish Rite
by Charles T. McClenachan
Softcover 616 pages
ISBN 1-934935-62-X

The Bonseigneur Rituals
Edited by Gerry L. Prinsen
Foreword by Michael R. Poll
8x10 Softcover 2 volumes 574 pages
ISBN 1-934935-34-4

Outline of the Rise and Progress of Freemasonry in Louisiana
by James B. Scot
Introduction by Alain Bernheim
Afterword by Michael R. Poll
8x10 Softcover 180 pages
ISBN 1-934935-31-X

The Life Story Of Albert Pike
by Fred W. Allsopp
6x9 Softcover 156 pages
ISBN 1-453756-87-6

Chapter Rose Croix
by Albert Pike
Foreword by Albert Mackey
6x9 Softcover 108 pages
ISBN 1-453762-02-7

Cornerstone Book Publishers
www.cornerstonepublishers.com

More Books in the Cornerstone Scottish Rite Education Series

The Ancient and Accepted Scottish Rite in Thirty-Three Degrees
by Robert B. Folger
Introduction by Michael R. Poll
6x9 Softcover 814 pages
ISBN: 1-934935-88-3

Egyptian Masonic Rite of Memphis
by Calvin C. Burt
6x9 Softcover 352 pages
ISBN: 1-613420-45-5

Historical Inquiry into the Origins of the Ancient and Accepted Scottish Rite
by James Foulhouze
Foreword by Michael R. Poll
6x9 Softcover 216 pages
ISBN 1-613420-26-9

The Schism Between the Scotch & York Rites
by Charles Laffon de Ladébat
6x9 Softcover 66 pages
ISBN 1-934935-33-6

The Grand Orient of Louisiana
A Short History and Catechism of a Lost French Rite Masonic Body
Introduction by Michael R. Poll
Softcover 52 pages
ISBN 1-934935-23-9

More Books in the Cornerstone
Scottish Rite Education Series

The Story of the Scottish Rite Lodge of New Orleans
Published with the Louisiana Lodge of Research
Edited by Gerry L. Prinsen
Introduction by Michael R. Poll
8.5x11 Softcover 194 pages
ISBN 1-613420-30-7

Éliphas Lévi and the Kabbalah
by Robert L. Uzzel
6 x 9 Softcover 208 pages
ISBN: 1-887560-76-9

Bibliography of the Writings of Albert Pike
by William L. Boyden
6x9 Softcover 88 pages
ISBN 1-453875-51-4

Morals and Dogma of the Scottish Rite Craft Degrees
by Albert Pike
Foreword by Michael R. Poll
6x9 Softcover 152 pages
ISBN 1-887560-86-6

Readings XXXII
Instructions in the Thirty-Second Degree
by Albert Pike
6x9 Softcover 174 pages
ISBN 1-453821-04-X

Cornerstone Book Publishers
www.cornerstonepublishers.com

CPSIA information can be obtained at www.ICGtesting.com
Printed in the USA
LVOW042258240812

295841LV00002B/2/P